The Dictionary of Unspellable Noises

Other books by Clint McCown

NOVELS

The Member-Guest
War Memorials
The Weatherman
Haints

POETRY

Labyrinthiad
Sidetracks
Wind Over Water
Dead Languages
Total Balance Farm

The Dictionary

of

Unspellable Noises

New & Selected Poems

1975 – 2018

Clint McCown

Press 53
Winston-Salem

Press 53, LLC
PO Box 30314
Winston-Salem, NC 27130

First Edition

Cover design by Clint McCown, Dawn Cooper,
and Kevin Morgan Watson

Cover art, "Fire," Copyright © 2015
by Clint McCown, used by permission of the artist

Author photo by Dawn Cooper

Library of Congress Control Number
2018953962

Printed on acid-free paper
ISBN 978-1-941209-88-2

for Dawn
again and always

and for Caitlin and Mallie
bright stars in any sky

My thanks to the editors of the following journals where versions of these poems appeared:

Alabama Literary Review: "Bird as Metaphor for Bird"
Alaska Quarterly Review: "Total Balance Farm"
Arts & Letters: "Modern Cartography"
Ascent: "Southern Comfort"
Bellingham Review: "Advice from the Previous Century"
Bluefish: "Poetics"
Burnside Review: "Two Infatuations, Two Red Cars, and an Allegory"
College English: "A Ten-Year-Old Boy Discovering the Certainty of Descent"
Colorado Review: "Graduation Speech for My Daughters"
Dan River Anthology: "Cemetery"
Eclipse: "Boring Sunset West of Fort Stockton, after a Storm"
Fifth Wednesday Journal: "Today's Lessons in the Animal Kingdom"
The Gettysburg Review: "Sarah Unbroken"
Hawaii Review: "American Highways," "Leftover Wishes," "On Thinking There Are Too Many Ways to Start a Poem about Death"
Hotel Amerika: "The First Morning in My New Apartment"
Kansas Quarterly: "Wind Over Water"
Louisville Review: "The Idea of Order in Key Largo," "In the Last Smiling Photo of My Mother"
Makeout Creek: "Autumn Rising"
New Orleans Review: "Still Life with Strings"
Nimrod: "Contemporary Doxology"
North American Review: "Instructions"
Numero Cinq: "Knock, Knock," "On Claudia's Birthday," "Entropy"
Poetry Daily: "Crossing Braddock Run"
Poetry Now: "Columbus," "In the Nursing Home," "The History of America," "Sidetracks," "Flesh Eaters on Parade"
Puerto del Sol: "Latin Class Foreshadows a Separation"
River Styx: "Why We Don't Look Forward to Eternal Damnation"
The Sewanee Review: "The Weather of the Game"
Snake Nation Journal: "Buying a New Motorcycle at Fifty"
Snake Nation Review: "The Night Marvin Gaye Was Shot by His Father," "Leaving Denver by Train"
Southern Poetry Review: "The Night before the Operation," "Splitting Up the Record Collection"

The Southern Review: "What I Should Know by Now,"
  "Questionnaire"
Sycamore Review: "The Right Answers in Middle America"
Tampa Review: "Waiting for the Next Ice Age," "Ten Haiku About
  the Limitations of the Heart, with One Missing"
Verse Daily: "Sarah, Unbroken"
Yearbook of American Poetry: "The Night before the Operation"

My thanks to the following editors and presses, where most of
these poems appeared in book form: Richard Spiegel at Bard
Press; Emily Wilson at Jackpine Press; Robert Olmsted at
Northwoods Press; Rick Campbell at Anhinga Press; and Kevin
Morgan Watson at Press 53.

Additional thanks for the relentless inspiration and support
provided by these poet and writer friends along the way: Keith
Ratzlaff, Jeff Gundy, Kevin Stein, David Wojahn, David Jauss,
Bret Lott, Mary Ruefle, Dean Young, Betsy Scholl, Mark Cox,
Ralph Angel, Matthew Dickman, Cynthia Huntington, Baron
Wormser, Jean Valentine, Connie May Fowler, Ellen Lesser,
Dick Bausch, Ron Carlson, Bai Dao, Dennis Lehane, Bob Butler,
Scott Sanders, Amber Timmerman, and, now absent, Archie
Ammons, Ursula LeGuin, Bill Stafford, Peter Matthiessen, Ray
Carver, and Claudia Emerson.

And to some people who have kept my raft afloat: Curt
Musselman & Cecelia Brown, Jim Frazee, John Rice, Dave
Pickering, Bob Hoylman, Pete Hull, Charlie and Bev Cooper,
Della Condon, Kevin Harland, and the whole Strong family,
especially Doug & Teresa, Lynn, Cindy, Pat (Pee-Wee), and Tom.

Contents

TODAY'S LESSONS IN THE ANIMAL KINGDOM

FLESH EATERS ON PARADE

INVOKING WHATEVER COMES NEXT

Boil an artichoke.
Compare the
prickly leaf tip
to the soft,
pale taste
of the heart,
a bitterness
so pure it isn't
bitter anymore.

Take the worst
thing that ever
happened to you
and say it
in ten words.
Then take
ten words away.
Think what's left.

We never see it coming, not really—
because we don't know what it is.
The jumper from the bridge is just

as unprepared as the pedestrian
stepping from the curb. We're all
oblivious to the water, its mysterious

depths; we're all oblivious to the bus,
its mysterious schedule and destination.
If there were clues along the way, we

missed them, thinking some eccentric
thought instead. That's the trouble
with simple truth—it can hide in a

shoebox, a teacup, a broken branch.
It can hide in the way we fail to look
at one another on the street, or the way

we stare at roadkill we can't identify.
Sure, some things we figure out—
we know that if our hands are cold

it doesn't help to stick them in the fire.
But we'll press the same button on
the elevator, day after day, forgetting

there's no guarantee we'll make it to
our floor. Ignore those idiot monks
who mummify themselves. Ignore

evangelists in shiny suits and all those
desperate salesmen trained to smile.
It's not your soul's salvation they have

in mind, it's their own car payments,
their own dreams of bigger homes.
Plumb the gaps between their carefully

articulated words, and you can hear their
hearts screaming out the same reality as
yours: that one day, without warning,

there'll be nothing left, not a single
thought, not a single heartbeat, not a
single breath. Only the search is endless,

as every generation proves, so try your
faith on that. Scan the dark world for
color and grace. Imagine music: let it

move you inward to the rhythms that
connect blood with bone. Sing every
strain that rises up inside. Keep dancing.

Abracadabra

In the cave we hunched low,
our backs to the cold wall,
grunting and snarling across the fire.
When there was sadness,
we cried sadness in a broken gush;
we laughed our happiness
whenever happiness came.
When night brought stillness,
our wakeful minds reached out:
we made up sounds
for *rock*, for *stick*, for *day*.

Our caves have plumbing now,
and here we are at *ennui*, here
we are at *paradigm*, here we are
at *antidisestablishmentarianism*.
Words settle like fallout on the lawn,
the residue of ages, layered on,
syllable by syllable, as needed,
as agreed upon. We taught
ourselves to speak histories,
then to embellish histories.
We shaped legends, then myths.

Language didn't teach us how to lie.
Every animal trap is a falsehood.
So, too, the first knotted club,
the first spear, the first tactic
to take an enemy by surprise.
The first bowing down.
The first kiss that meant nothing.
The first unspoken longing,
and the second, and the last.

We were born to mislead, and
language mimicked our deceptions
from the nursery on. No dog
has ever barked *bow-wow*.
There is no *cock-a-doodle-doo*.
Bang is tragically wrong for the gun.

When I was ten
I learned from comic books
that people falling from a great height
yelled *Aieeeeee!* all the way down,
and I accepted that on faith until
I stumbled on a housetop and
fell myself, silent as a sack of grain.

Language unspools across time,
while experience arrives all at once,
a hailstorm blowing in from all directions,
battering the senses.
Sometimes there isn't room for words.

Like beauty, truth is easier to see than say,
easier to hear, feel, smell, and taste.
If a tree falls in the forest, no alphabet
can parse the silence from the sound.
The screamer never knows
the spelling of the scream.

We know the noise the drinking straw
makes draining drops from a glass,
the jar shattering on pavement,
the coin spinning on the countertop,
the wheeled suitcase rolling along
the terminal floor. We know
the reverberation of the diving board
when the large man launches himself
high above water, the sound
of water parting when he comes down.

But language is more cloud than stone.
The *squeal* of tires on wet pavement
is not the *squeal* of the young girl
getting the bike she wanted, or
the *squeal* of a pig in the slaughterhouse.

Moses sought the name of God
but got a dodgy answer.

Maybe phonics was the catch,
the word unspellable as a car horn.
Maybe the sound of God
is too long to say in a single life.
Maybe the sound of God is imaginary
and therefore uncontainable.
Maybe the sound of God
is different every time.

Out in the yard the dandelion
folds its yellow petals at dusk,
then reopens at dawn,
a different thing entirely,
a miracle of fresh architecture,
a constellation of ghosts
ready to be lifted up. We pine
for that same alchemy, the power
to spin ourselves from straw to gold,
to talk our way past the tall gates.
We take hopeful hyperbolic leaps,
claiming to leave footprints on the sun;
but that's another lie.

Existence writes its own dictionary
and language is just a game we play
to keep the clocks ticking, and to
reassure ourselves of kinship with
the world. But kinship is a hope at best,
and nature is sealed up inside itself,
deaf to all vocabularies but its own.
There's no breaching that ancient door,
no cracking the code of
unintended symbols, no solving the
riddle of an old stone lion in the sand.

In every dream we buy the wrong
textbook, study for the wrong exam,
sweat it out in the back row
stealing each other's wrong answers.
Then the bell rings, and we're left with

nothing for the trophy case,
nothing to put in the black frame
and fasten to the wall. We might as well
be tongue-tied, for all we fail to say.

But words don't bow out gracefully.
We gripe about the price of limousines,
then sing sad songs about
what's missing from the heart.

Outside, maybe the floodwaters rise,
or maybe termites gut that
load-bearing wall in the kitchen,
but we miss the signs,
we're off somewhere naming
the unnameable. So while Rome
and all the other empires burn,
our list of words expands through
every subtle shade of meaning,
plumping out a scrapbook we hope—
that word again—to be remembered by.

We teach our children *rock*, and *stick*,
and *day*, and soon they think there
must be words for everything,
as we ourselves once thought.

Illusion: that's the magic we possess,
and spell becomes a word of incantation.
Abracadabra, we might say,
I create what I speak. That's the comfort
we keep hidden up our sleeve.
A white dove, an ace of diamonds,
a string of colored handkerchiefs
with no end in sight.
Anything bright and unexpected will do.
Anything to distract us from the dark.

The old church three farms down
the road burned to the ground.

Now it's a charred scar on a small
rise, nothing left of it but history

and a homeless congregation. But
someone will donate a scraggly

patch a few miles up the highway,
and they'll rebuild. It's what we

all do when day capsizes into night,
when the whirlwind comes, or the

flood, or in this case lightning.
Even so, buildings don't matter

in the end. The body is a stain
upon the soul, or so they say, and

at times I see the logic. Nature
drives a one-sided bargain, and it's

tough to know where we fit in.
Deer and deer ticks flourish as

much as possum or raccoon, but
we're out of step, killing on impulse

like the lone cat or, worse, the
pack-bound dog. At Total Balance

Farm the horses come and go,
the hawk watches, the weather

changes. Cobwebs coated in stall
dust hang like silk stockings from

the barn rafters. The riding ring
offers up seashells after a rain,

the remnants of an ancient time.
I wish I could say what life is like

in this place of shelter and sudden
dangers, but language fails to

measure up, even to the ordinary.
The more a word is used, the

less it means, so some things we
take on faith, like displaced

congregants continuing the habit
of prayer. Any piece of land is

holy if we name it so. You think
seeing is believing? Humans

know the moon has no light of its
own. But it still beats the darkness.

I

In my teens I would have made
            a good evangelist,
juiced on hormones, wiry and

determined, loud enough to pitch
            my voice to the
rafters, dumb enough to tell

a stranger what to think;
            and I still see
hints of revelation and rapture

in the way every screw untightens
            itself over time,
rising against gravity. But I've

also seen those photos of distant
            nebulae shrouded
in pink fluorescent gasses,

looking like membranes from the
            delivery room floor;
misshapen galaxies that may have

vanished eons before the first
            postcard arrived.
There's no telling what's out there.

We're alive somehow in a field of
            shifting coordinates, and
I'm too torn between architectures

to cheerlead for anybody's
            collection plate.
Gone keeps coming to mind.

Even locally: good health is just
          a delaying tactic.
My father used to say his knees

were killing him, but that's not
          what killed him.
You know how it is, a thing

gradually takes on weight, then the
          load shifts and suddenly
you're jack-knifed on the highway.

II

Every image is a story and every
          story answers a
question. The early Choctaw

shaped a legend of great ragged
          mountains in the west,
calling them the backbone of the

world. That's fine with me:
          land or sky,
geography is always the best

compass point for myth. But I
          take things more
personally. Here's a New York

story: my friend Russell went
          uptown for a game
of chess and got stabbed instead.

Here's a North Carolina story:
          my friend Rick's heart
gave out. Life is life sometimes.

III

And every story raises a question.
        Are pivotal moments
inevitable? If David's aim had

failed him, would Goliath have
        just stood there
until the damned boy got it right?

Probably not, and that's how
        fragile history can be.
We each have our own mysteries

to fall back on. I'd like to know
        what happened to
all those silver graduation pens.

I'd like to know the last safe
        place on earth.
And what if the thing you're most

afraid of is sleep? What if you
        never make anyone
proud? What if we aren't dead

until all the chaos we contributed
        has run its course,
which means not anytime soon?

What if logic goes out the window
        even in a room
with no windows? What if love

turns out to be a snapping turtle—
        do we pray for thunder?
The trouble is, my ideas are all over

the map, and the map's been in the
        glove compartment
too long. New roads have been laid

out, and I'm left with limitations.
        I was a grown man
before I knew concrete gave off heat

as it hardened. I used to yearn
        for bosses to
thank me. If there's an *et cetera*

involved, I don't want to hear it.
        Nevertheless I
have beliefs: that civilization

wasn't born in a teacup; that no
        species can rule
the world without a good skeletal

system; that there's more to
        contemplation's bottom
line than, *Here we are at last.*

You think you need an afterlife?
        Okay, but what if
it's a ransacked closet in the

back room of a burgled house in
        a bad neighborhood?
What if it's a rusty bucket of

discontinued paint? What if it's
        the same old voice
saying, *Well, what did you expect?*

It doesn't help
to jump a freight,
lie back in moonlight
on loose straw, and
pretend homelessness;

or that home
is the clattering, winding
curve of rails
icing a thin way.

Cold stirs up
through the tin floor and
whips through gaps in the
boxcar slats. The mind

leapfrogs away, says
the tumbleweed travels
but seldom grows,
calls mushrooms
harbingers of damp hope,
toadstools
the vaudeville of vegetation,

leaps again
to draw the line on those
who pose by windows
and recite, leaps last
to a sculptor
imagining a stone so perfect
it needs no chiseling on.

Do something right. Stand all day
in a bright field throwing a boomerang
against the wind. Let it come back.

Don't be distracted by whatever's ticking
in your DNA. Ignore the burning car
on 4th Street by the river. The brain will

assert kinship, but that's nothing new.
Even between a blow to the head and
blacking out, there's room for comment.

While papers pile up on the doorstep,
divert yourself with natural problems:
the perfect throw eventually goes nowhere.

Examine the gray metaphysics of routine.
Walking the dog, mowing the yard.
Responsibility is invisible, no hook

or claw, nothing but pure weight,
but maybe you handle it, maybe you
already know you can't spend your life

taking hot showers. Carry this knowledge
to the hardware store, the gas station,
the mall, the Piggly Wiggly. Don't answer

merely out of habit: the future needs
all kinds, sometimes paper, sometimes
plastic. The crowd splits neatly into

desperations: those who want out and
those who want in. Consider going it
alone. Buy a ticket to a place you've

never been, watch seals from an excursion
boat. Discover the ancient pleasure
of knowing where you are on a map,

of locating yourself in a signified
landscape. Smile at that illusion of
certainty. And if after all this you're

still foolish enough to want to measure
yourself, don't do it against whatever
mountain lies around the river's bend.

No pearls, no precious stones.
Just granite from the abandoned quarry,
rough cut and fissured. Not much use at all.

Hope
is another embarrassment.
I'd do the impossible if I could,
or at least the unlikely.
I'd call down the hawk from the pine,
I'd explain the difference
between the darkness of the cave
and the darkness at the center of the sun.
I'd crowbar my speech into a frame of mind
that hasn't been framed before.

But what can I say? You know
as much as I do. We're equally unique,
equally as common as breath.
We see the same blue sky,
suffer, laugh, long for the unreachable.
We've all plucked needles from our hearts.
We've all seen the enemy smile.

So what if our parents were
chain-smoking alcoholics wielding
leather belts, or whatever stark scene
your stunted childhood might have been?
We're still around.
So what if there was damage?

My dog
is really my wife's dog, though
I named him. He often looks worried.
If he's busy, he pretends he doesn't
hear my call. But I control the word
that set's him whirling by the door: *ball*.
Retrieving is the only game he knows.
He'll cross most boundaries for *ball*.

My life has no equivalent.
I never whirl, except in secret.
My games are cold, rooted in habit
and arcane beliefs. Schools have
taught me how to fetch, but
all my knowledge has an expiration date.
I see my moments fade
into a lengthening line of ghosts.

About the afterlife: the rumor persists.
And why not?
We've known conception and birth,
twin passages that ended in surprise.
Who can say what's next?

Make your best guess and call it religion,
that's how we operate,
some so afraid of being wrong
they kill the doubters.

The Buddhists advocate emptiness,
but what they mean is
don't buy that new car or the big TV.
Right for the spirit, wrong for the economy.

At least they understand
the kinship of opposites—
that yin and yang are not divisible,
that the unseeing eye
and the all-seeing eye
are essentially the same.

There are things I could say about emptiness,
but I won't, which is a zen approach.

By heritage I'm Reformed Presbyterian,
which means I no longer burn witches.
I married one, in fact, when I was young—
a novice Wiccan who stirred our

simmering cauldron for two years
then wisely put me on the street.
Another emptiness.

The sky starts with emptiness,
that baseline blue,
but its nature is infinite, always changing,
never the same sky twice.
That's why we keep watching,
even at night,
when stars give us reason
to wonder without ceasing.

Whether spurred by God or dog,
we chase things in the mind—
that rented textbook where every question
is a math problem at heart.
Check your worksheet for examples:
Be *fruitful and multiply*, says the Black Book,
Divide and conquer, says Julius Caesar,
Just add water, says Betty Crocker.

And don't forget the writing
on the playground wall:
Billy + Suzy, Johnny + Jill,
all those seventh grade mysteries
summed up by love, equations
held in balance by a long line
of irrational and imaginary numbers.

Is each galaxy shaped like a virus,
or is each virus shaped like a galaxy?
The answer always surprises me.

So what do we have besides our loss
of innocence, of faith, of self-respect?
Even hope is a subset of disappointment,
a wish to retrieve something,
to regain that rounded wholeness
in which we once believed.

Now there's a belief
for every decimal place in Pi.

And what is Pi?
An ironic, endless number—
the one we use to calculate
the volume of the ball.

Invoking Whatever Comes Next   1978

excerpt from "Wind Over Water" from *Wind Over Water*

My mind has been misled too long
to know the old roads anymore.
I now invent a different course:
dissolve my blood,
dispense it to the wind in clouds
that storm wild
to pull the old, dry waters up
and spin them into leaner, darker
oceans of the air;
black circling forms that
push beyond the prehistoric dreams
of fish and fishers, inland,
where the oldest seabirds
blow away to die.
Here cold thoughts fall frozen
to the ground and crystallize
in psalms that sing the altitude.

I would draw the dream
within the dream
and set its figure in the cold smoke
of this timber morning,
high up where the sun burns wet
between the broken bark and leaves.
I would set the dark or
near-dark loose
around it on the mountainside
to keep it braced for clarity and
coming warm decay. I would
draw the dream out from the dream,
shape it in the long dark, and
set it on the mountaintop like noon.

But even here the mind is not all
that it should be:
morning rime hangs on too long,
the haze of old haunts
haunts me through the senses—
a face under a faucet, say,

or a pool room I once lost in—
then passes on before the reflex
quickens, thaws, dissolves.
So: the memory doesn't quite jog;
the glass stays darkly. I see
a thing I won't remember seeing.

Still, this place will do me for
a while. Elsewhere, I am the face
in broken glass. I am in the light
too bright and the dark too deep.
I am not quite the physicist. I am
the misfit everywhere but here.

AMERICAN HIGHWAYS

Walking in Baltimore, my pace driven by a
salt-wind that scoured the inner harbor streets,
I passed a building with a banner on its side
that said
   Believe
I listened for the whistling flutter of quail
breaking for the night trees, heard only
the tight crunch of shallow snow.

Across the empty lots from Camden Yards,
a thin man hailed me from the dark and
poured out the detailed story of his loss.
The cops, he said, had been no help at all.
His wallet and his duffle bag were gone.
He needed cash
to make the hundred miles back home.

I'd heard this con before
another cold night, another city street.
I knew already the slow progress of ice
through the sleeping mind and the long odds
against us. I told him I was too old now
to put much credence in his steady gaze.
He sighed, and asked again.

All gifts are temporary. The wool cap,
the leather belt, the chill, the light, the breath,
the moving hand. Not worthless, though.

I'll pay you back, he swore—which was enough,
I guess, stuck as we are in this middle passage
between extremes of dust and ash.

Crossing Braddock Run

On the far bank
      of Braddock Run
      in high summer
   you might find
   the deep satisfaction

primal
elemental
   of crossing quick water
   after a rain

It might not be easy

   Around your footing
nothing will lurk
but steady and
      irregular force

   the stones worn smooth
   and slippery
the shallow
     shattering
   surface of the run
   alive
   with imbalance
in the mottled
     morning light

Take a slow breath
   feel
the cool air
   of the shallows

   hear
the small water sounds
    rising

Look briefly back
then climb the rough bank
          if you can

and look closely
          at the hydrangea's

pink flower
     blue flower
          white flower
Forget
     your life's obsession
with decay

Everything
          in the natural world
     is driven by beauty

We have much
          to live up to

I'm supposed to know better. I've camped
already in that purgatory of magnified
mistakes all cyclists dread. I've propped
my boots on the cold yellow couches

outside neurosurgery, marking time among
the hard-luck remains of oil-stained
families in Grateful Dead tee-shirts, all of
us waiting our turn for news, all of us

hoping for unlikely results. The vending
machines looked cheerful, but the candy
bars were stale. Still, we bummed change
from the night nurses or the green-scrubbed

orderlies as they wheeled their carts of
clean linens silently down the hall. Mostly
what we talked about was other crashes,
the litany of failed maneuvers that left so

many dark spots on the highway. Our tone
hovered in the ordinary, hushed, matter-of-
fact, as if loss were a common accessory,
affordable, standard as polished chrome.

In hospitals every bystander becomes
an expert in the hard sciences, learns that
physics always beats biology, that when
a body goes from sixty to zero in a heartbeat,

the heart won't beat anymore. The brain
snaps from its stalk like cauliflower, and
all a helmet does is make an open casket
possible. Forget horsepower. When a hose

breaks, everything stops, no matter the
complexity around it. But what corner
doesn't have death holding up a lamppost?
A man with a slipped disc can freeze in a

bathtub. Heatstroke can kill a healthy
woman bringing folding chairs down from
the attic. The body looks for ways to turn
against us. The cramp in deep water.

The malignant growth, inoperable and
spreading. The giving up and the shutting
down. Coach said walk it off, but some
roads don't stretch far enough. I watched

my parents both blink out with big diseases.
I found my cat lying stiff in its own urine.
A sign on Interstate 70 near Columbus
says *Resume Legal Speed*, but sometimes

fresh momentum is hard to come by.
A body at rest tends to remain a body.
I've seen other signs as well: the morning
of my great-grandmother's funeral I sat

with well-dressed grown-ups in her
front parlor and stared through dusty
slants of light at fruit pieces trapped in
Jell-O. Everything I said was wrong.

There's something good about sinking a
shovel into soft earth, or starting a tractor
in tall weeds, or lodging an axe blade
solidly in wood. I open up the throttle

on an empty road at night, accelerating
into the small pool of what's visible.
We've all got that one scary moment up
ahead, so why not set impossible standards?

On a scale of one-to-ten, I give infinity a
nine, eternity a seven, the universe a three.
Bereavement barely registers. *Stick with
what you know* is a motto for the dead, so I've

tried to cover ground. A veteran survivor
of two wrecks in my teens, two more in
my twenties, I've crossed the Brooklyn Bridge
and the Golden Gate, Texas and Death

Valley. I've run the dunes at Kitty Hawk
and Coney Island, and the Dragon's
Tail in Tennessee. I've dragged the littered
beach flats at Daytona. I broke down

once in Truth or Consequences and got
a mild concussion outside Santa Fe.
I rode with Hell's Angels up the California
coast. I've driven that sad tree-tunnel

they sometimes put on post cards, passing
through the redwood's butchered heart.
There's always some level of grief beyond
our own, and nothing in the cosmos

drives defensively. The brain may calm
itself with math problems, but life depends
on motor skills. Left or right, up or down,
pedal or fall over, we saddle ourselves

with the ping-pong of binary options.
Our metaphysics hinges on true or false,
dead or alive, heaven or hell. Either
the mind ends in a snapshot or it doesn't.

My computer thinks any word it doesn't
know is a misspelling, because that's the
choice we gave it. By now I've forgotten
the difference between nightmare and

dream, am not dismayed by the crate of
scorpions uncovered in my trunk. *Who
put them there?* I wonder. The shorthand
seems familiar, but the message always

fades. God will not do our dirty laundry.
We're people, and we live in miles per
hour between evaporating worlds of
blood and dead languages, innocent of

the crimes at hand, but punishable in
general. Where I still choose to live, an old
ink spill stains my bed sheet, as if sleep
has drained a blackness from my chest.

Details are more visible from the darker of two
rooms, if two rooms are what you're left with.

It's a rainy day in Vermont, and I'm sick with
fever. I've flooded my system with usual juices,

various pills; friends have left remedies at my
door. Still, my brain stutters like old film slipping

from its sprockets. I see Bob Ford shooting Jesse
James in the back, and somehow I'm Bob Ford,

I'm Jesse James. The picture stays crooked forever.
Speaking in tongues, the electric fan swivels to face

me, then cooly turns away. My mind bombards
itself with song fragments I despise. None of this

is voluntary. I know I ought to rest, but exercise
has carnival colors, grab-bags filled with dime-store

surprises, and sure enough, on the downhill walk
to town, I see a black car covered in pink rain-beaten

petals. The whispered hush of tires on wet asphalt
comes and goes, familiar as the double yellow line.

A small thing, this ease of recognition, but
comforting; and if optimism weren't already on

its hands and knees scrubbing toilets at the bus
station, I'd feel inclined to roll with the landscape,

turn somersaults and cartwheels, let gravity guide
me down. But I'm not crazy. I know that

"Singin' in the Rain" is a fine musical number
but a poor life strategy. The gutters here are rough

and not suitable for dancing. Moreover, I'm short
on choreography. Across the avenue an oversized

granite wall banks the hillside. A mudslide lurks
back there somewhere, drumming its fingers, but

for now the gray blocks hold the line, sturdy
as the Middle Ages. My own middle ages are

more reflective of the moment, green leaves bobbing
in the silvery runoff, slipping through the sewer's

gaping grate. When I was ten I pinned a towel
to my shirt, climbed my cousin's roof, and took

a running leap, believing I could fly. I floated briefly
on the breeze and tumbled like a feather through

the summer grass. A decade later, I lived in New
York City on forty dollars a week—another kind

of floating. Now my foot on the pavement is less
certain, a scientist's probe testing for ruptures.

My mind is cut glass, refracting what it already
knows: that civilization is a highway with few

exits, and the past precedes us everywhere we
go. Pinpricks of sweat cover my neck and scalp.

I pause by a utility pole and focus on the sagging
rooftops of the town, think leveling thoughts

to coax my pulse back slowly from the ledge.
But that's okay, we all get winded in the long run.

We're built for speed, not distance, and even
the gods overexert themselves, always pulling

up lame in the closing lap. The smart money
allows for breakdown. Among today's discoveries:

community can cure most common ills, but the
world shows best in isolation; a tree can buckle

long after the storm; people often mistake freedom
for happiness, happiness for love, love for a pack

mule. After the rain a cool breeze carries fragrances
pure enough to shame the heart. Steam rises like

prayer from the washed streets, and the sun carves
a broken shadow through the town. I take it all in.

Sunday evenings at the dump
I toss whatever's broken or
irrelevant. It's never easy.
No one wants to call a thing
unsalvageable. But what good
is a splintered axe handle,
a rotted ladder, a cracked bucket?

Why save machine parts
after the machines are gone,
or stacks of roofing shingles
thick with moss and mold, or
sacks of concrete hardened
into stone? Forget history, that
cesspool of nostalgia and regret.
The world says usefulness
is a here-and-now affair,
the opposite of what's eternal.
Worn out is a death sentence
even for the faithful, and
pointless is a point of no return.

I like the ride home, the truck bed
empty, my life free of waste.
But in the rear-view mirror I
see what lies ahead: everything
thought, everything written,
everything that once blazed
brightly or amazed.

Just after the last fork,
even the highway turns to dust.

Columbus

When he got back
nobody said
tell us how round things are
they just said
where's the gold?

and when he answered
this is bamboo
you can make
whistles from it
they shook their heads
and pegged him
(too late)
for a bad risk

a foreigner
adrift somewhere
between the edge
of the world
and the going price
of discovery

The History of America

America was not discovered, it was
invented by a research marketer
who ran it up the flagpole and

gauged its saluteability ratio at
nine-point-seven, which was
very good, profit-projection-wise, so

he mounted it on wheels to make it
look like a bandwagon, fed it apple
pies, and even played baseball

on it to demonstrate its versatility;
but according to the surveys it
still wasn't slick enough to fool

all the people all the time, so he
covered it with plastic gizmos,
propped the whole thing up on

Golden Arches, and taught it how
to spin wood from aluminum. The
people were understandably impressed

and America sold like hotcakes;
and the first two hundred and fifty
million paying customers received

Absolutely Free a long-playing
record of small birds singing
from the stomach of a cat.

American Highways

1984

There are things
we do not go back for:
the roadmap, say,
refolded on the pump;
the old umbrella
raveling from its spokes,
forgotten on a toilet door;
the red windbreaker
on the café chair, recalled
too late, too dark,
an hour down the road.

Speed lures us
into strange beliefs.

We hit the interstate's
long stride,
slipstream into the
white blur of travel.

Transformers line
a shriveled ditch.
A ghost creek
feels its way by wire.

Ahead, we look
for signs, for exits with
the services we need.
Remembering,
we curse ourselves
and take the loss.

The Idea of Order in Key Largo 2002

The storm descends like gangsters
muscling in. Waves maul the shore,
wind becomes wall, chaos howls
at every window, every door.

We wait inside with what we know:
intensities don't last. But when a
gale can drive a broom straw
through the brain, better to lie low.

Green times at heart, wondering
if the roof will hold, if nature
really takes the killer's side.

Who wouldn't fall in love, sip
drinks at the hotel bar, stare down
a stranger with a dangerous past?

We're all professionals here,
pale faces posed in the flickering
light. We take direction naturally.

Meanwhile, the B reels accumulate.
In one, an ex-wife shrieks over dirty
laundry. A mother threatens suicide.
A father whistles light tunes while
fatal illness blossoms in his brain.
A daughter screams from wreckage
on the highway, "What's happening
to me? What's happening to me?"

In every story, *once* becomes
forever, as bad-takes curl
upon the cutting room floor.
What's left is what we pay to see:
a tale spooled out in increments,
unlayering itself like
celluloid transparencies
from an anatomy text, revealing

something deeper than a name.
Peel back the image frame by frame:
here we see the scarring, here
the web of nerves, here the cage
of bone beneath a rush of blood,
here the quickening heart.
The mind casts about for some
bird-like glimmer, a cry
from the trees, a low swoop
across a scorched lawn.

Somewhere, *Once upon a time*.
Somewhere else, darkness.

Transportation

The lure of the cruise
is slow deliberation

the long, drawn feeling
of movement
compassed by a drag
beyond control

plodding
like the calm, calm,
beating of the blood

the sea rain
hangs in beads on
porthole glass

disappearing lightly

in the glare

replanting
in the blue squints
of passengers

After the Frost

Three hundred and sixty roads diverged
where the woods were cut down to
accommodate them all; and looking
out across the white, flat horizon,
I had no idea what might or might not

be a reasonable choice of direction.
One road seemed pretty much the same
as any other: they were all paved,
well-lit, and clearly marked, courtesy
of the coordinated efforts of the State

Highway Commission and the State Depart
ment of Corrections. But looking ahead
to the time when I've pulled into a
pungent tile rest stop to eat my pimento
cheese sandwich at a concrete roadside

table, I don't sigh and wonder what my
sandwich would have been if I had set
my motion at another angle to the wind.
The directions vary, but they're all
still spokes of the same bound wheel.

Boring Sunset West of Fort Stockton,
   after a Storm   2005

Choose your light well.

Maybe everything starts out fine,
then one day she hands you a list, says
If we ever split up, this is what I'm keeping.
It's downhill from there.
At some point camping seems a good idea.
The wilderness overtakes you.

Scrub trees punctuate the badland plains,
trunks bowed hard by the prevailing wind,
branches the crippled shape of prayer.
A pure form of memory.
The red sand, too, holds every passing sign.

The wind has swept up through the buttes
and landed black in the north sky.

You notice the stillness, how impatient a
silent landscape seems. At dusk the rocks
lean toward their shadows, waiting.

A land of cruel resemblances,
where ragged edges flourish,
sharpened and heat-beaten.

Split bone arrives more native here
than flesh. Never mind
what's circling overhead.

Back home, where truth nails its joke
to both sides of the door,
the hardest thing to throw away
is the garbage can.
Ideals are ladders to fall from,
and every crack in the pavement
sprouts fire ants and weeds.

So you sit blindly in the holy nowhere
of mesas and arroyos, the new tent up,

the gear stowed dry, thinking
there ought to be a thing to say about
the sagebrush or the sunset worth
remembering. There isn't, though.

It's one more slow descent,
wide and gray behind the clouds;
dull, except to say
it darkens out more space, more land
than you have seen shut down before.
The sagebrush merely vanishes,
a minor shrug.

Above you the night scrawls out
more stars than there are words.
You'd like to hope for something,
but the sky is not a wishing well.

Old photos, a plaque with
your name on it, a bicycle you don't
remember buying, a Japanese sword,
an antique bonnet chest.

In the end, all mysteries are lists.

1.
mama, dada, pee-pee
three, four, five
yes
God and Jesus
please and thank you

2.
Columbus, 1492
Pilgrims, to escape religious persecution
taxation without representation
i before e
photosynthesis
a disappointed office seeker
the Pythagorean Theorem

3.
Yes, sir, officer
That wasn't me, officer
It won't happen again, officer

4.
I love you
I do
Itemized, filing jointly
This is delicious
We can't afford it
You don't look fat

5.
Must be Santa
That isn't yours
No
Because you could put an eye out
Because I said so
Maybe for your birthday

6.
I saw it on TV
I'll need another estimate
I'll do it tomorrow
We've grown apart

7.
something with fiber
God and Jesus
not lately
not anymore
not that I recall
call 911

Two Infatuations, Two Red Cars, and an Allegory

2006

1968: She lived in a small brick house
across the alley, and I could see her
bedroom window from my own. The
curtains were always drawn. In study
hall I dreamed pliers and hacksaws,
but the cage held, and I remained love's
lab rat in every class we shared. One day
that spring she took a fleeting interest
in my car, a red two-seater, and asked if
I would take her for a wild ride in the
rain. We spun out on a tight curve and
had to walk back into town. Fifteen years
later she was a part-time aerobics
instructor, and I saw her in a tavern
listening to her brother play lead guitar
in a local band. She remembered the ditch
that stranded us, but not me, not my name.

1969: The next car was more substantial,
with a steel roof and a cramped back
seat. But there was also another crush,
a girl one grade behind me, whose ring
finger had been bitten off by a zebra
at the Minneapolis Zoo. She asked me
to drown baby chicks in formaldehyde
for her science project. She got an A,
and I thought we were going steady
until I saw her at the movies with a
French horn player named Bob. I took
a detour home that night, accelerated to
sixty-five, and steered the car into a tree.

Ask any town cop and he'll tell you:
small red cars mean trouble. These
days I drive a white one. I rise early,
knowing every dawn cures a darkness.
I buy sturdy shoes and go for difficult
walks in the countryside, and I can tell
you this: if your feet hold out, as well

49

as your faith, there comes that point in
the hike when the stream you've been
expecting shows up gushing just like
you'd like it to; and if you keep your
balance long enough to wade the middle,
you'll find the water deep enough to
lie down in without bruising, shallow
enough so you don't get carried away.

I wanted to be a cowboy
     like my grandfather

become that lean horseman
     standing in front
     of the cigar store
   near the railway depot

     twirling a rope, a lariat
no chaps because they look stupid
     but yes, a pair of jangly
spurs on well-stitched boots

a silver buckle balancing
     a six-gun slung low
both glinting in the sun

       certainly a hat
       dusty white
not ten gallon, but smaller
    with a sharp crease
       and a curved brim
       more Colorado than Texas

my palomino idling
     by the hitching post
   flicking flies with its tail

nowhere special to go
   nowhere special
     I haven't already been

dust in the street
a dollar in my pocket

    that's all, that simple

    but
between the first ambition
and the last

        wind comes howling
down the arroyos
kicking up dust and
        reshaping the territory

something rattles
                        something strikes
                and suddenly cowboys
aren't
                what they used to be

the cutting horse
                dissects the herd

        life gets complicated

THE MEDITATION XVII BLUES

Birthright

When we arrive, pained and baffled, all
speech is mystery. Sure, we have some

basic answers in our blood, our bones,
whatever DNA provides. We breathe

without thinking. We generate a pulse;
consume, digest, expel. We sweat.

Cleave is our first instinct, and since the
mind has not yet learned to interfere

we know when to bind and when to sever.
Then words take shape, for ball, for door.

We cry the wish to be lifted up, the wish
to be fed, the wish to be comforted. Shades

of meaning cheat us out of certainty and
stutter the heart with vague directions home.

Only after years of dying in cold alleys
can we know that life is not a thing to be

conquered, or even put into words. Birth
is a passage we won't remember, and so is

death, but the middle is what matters.
We're more than just prisoners waiting to

be let out. We are the universe asking itself
a question. We are the part that wonders.

The bathtub overflows and we call it love,
though some problems are insoluble.

Say you've had your great-grandfather's
overstuffed armchair twenty-five years and
discovered that's long enough. Is the yard
sale a betrayal, or just a *deus ex machina* ending?

In our dreams we hide under porches when
the giants come and pray deliverance from
strangers whispering our name. The dark
river offers drowning in a salesman's voice,
the sky fills with sharpened wings.
There's much in every world to flee from.

A diseased opossum hisses in a garbage can
out back, a woman puts her hot ankle on mine
and tilts her head to touch my temple lightly,
a baby goat pulls at my pant leg, a jar of marbles
shatters from a shelf, a spider sac opens in the
night. There's no logical progression here.

In Latin class, I sat behind the beauty queen,
distracted every second as I conjugated verbs.

Amo, amas, amat, amamus, amatis, amant:
this much I still know.

But some things are untranslatable.
I'm tired of walking down highways of
beautiful women, tired of swallowing smoke
in God's bowling alleys. Life should be more
than the culmination of my worst mistakes.

Amo, ammo, the same word. I love
the stray bullet, the arrow through the heart.

But *absit invideo*, let there be no ill will,
though tragedies accumulate.
Exempli gratia, in Grand Central Station
a limping man with paper dolls to sell
calls out colors in a slurred voice.
His shoes pull him across the depot floor
like slow barges working upriver.

Sunt lacrimae rerum, there are tears for things.

Fine, if that's a notion you can use.
But every culture comes with limitations:
the Romans had no word for *picnic*.

Birds flock past a cathedral tower, moving
in loose concert, like a flag snapping in the
wind. A straggler follows them northward.

When a language is dead,
why do we still speak it?

Reality's Pool

The clear
       reflected edge
       held isolated

       lives through
the back of a photograph
       held
       to the light

such easy
       translocation

       gives the lie
   to the
       rigor
of reality:

       empirical translations
       of the
light-held world

are found no thicker
       than
       the depth
of an eyebeam
     at its turning point

fragile
and
    almost imaginary

A Rock and a Hard Place 1975

A man went looking
for the wind one day
to find the two extremes
of its existence;

and just as luck
or quick will
would have it
a sudden cracking gulf
broke loose
and gushed around him
with a wild
imaginary roar;

and sure enough
he caught the
full direction of its force
and yoked it soundly
to the quiet
at his back;

then as the wind washed up
into the sky again,
his mind encountered
two near-perfect thoughts:

one was about
eternity,
which he never finished,
and one was about
nothing,
which he never began

Entropy

Knowledge
is to understand
the differences;
wisdom
is to bridge
the common ground.

Suspenders and suspense,
for example:
shoulder to shoulder
but otherwise unattached.

Which is the one to learn from?

Even on our worst day
we can draw abstractions
from the concrete.
Even an unanchored
suspension bridge
can be easily supported
by the willing suspension
of our disbelief.

But abstractions leave us
none the wiser;
let's get practical here.

The river is beautiful only
until we have a need to cross it.

The river is ugly only
until we reach the other side.

Back and forth we go.

The earth is as much
pendulum as ball,
so even the peaceable kingdom
will know a day of slaughter.

And another.
And another.

Progress, it seems,
takes us nowhere
we haven't already been.

The river is beautiful,
the river is ugly,
but the river is not
the flooded landscape
or the drought-cracked bed.
The river is only the river.

The pendulum slows,
revealing every star as finite.

If left alone, every blade
unsharpens over time.
Every color fades toward
neutral, every fruit drops,
every drop dries.
Every strength falters,
every breath, every light
goes out, and every memory,
good or bad, is lost.

I am now here or
I am not here,
two states separated
by one letter,
one infinity of difference.

Fire reduces the bulk
of the universe to ash;
what's left will freeze
into atomic dust.

Don't wait for the sun
to fill the sky.
If there's a worm hole,
take it.

Remember that shade tree
in your old backyard.
You're there now. Stay a while.

The black widow nests
inside the glove:
things are set in motion

but feel
the bright passages
beforehand:

on a cool night
beer in a local bar
small talk between friends

conversations without war

or the next day:
the braces finally off,
a daughter's teeth
arranged in a new smile

sunshine, unnatural
this time of year

a bevy of quail rising
beyond the hunter's range,
a new dog from the pound,
a faded dollar
on the sidewalk

that dark tarpaper shack
we can't help
coming home to: hope

Some bet pollution stops the show,
some wager war.
Since greed has made us blind, I know
pollution is the way we'll go.
But still I get what bombs are for,
and fear has always run the race,
so maybe for extinction, war
could close the case
on either/or.

The next time
you're
trying to
     remember

exactly what
     it is
you've lost

remember this:

every
     thought
blade of grass

contributes
to the
          texture
     of direction

          accepting
the necessity
     of line

          and
bending
     just right

Not knowing what to think,
I went out to the pine forest
and asked a basic question:
is the mind a process or a thing?

I don't get your meaning, said the forest.

I suppose, I said,
what I really want to know
is if the spirit is separate from the body.

Oh, that again, said the forest,
bristling a few of its branches.
*Sorry to disappoint, but
superstitions are lost on me.*

But my question is real, I objected.

Only to you, said the forest.
And I'm not here to solve your insecurities.

Nevertheless, I said, I think
you may have information I can use.

Undoubtedly I do, replied the forest.
*Not to brag, but I have
a complete catalogue of every season.*

Then maybe you could share
a small secret or two, I said, so I
might understand what can't be seen.

No can do, sighed the forest,
standing firm.
I don't deal in hypotheticals.

I'm surprised you're so easily stumped,
I said, and the forest darkened.
A flight of birds flushed from the treetops.

Surely, I persisted,
with your vast knowledge
you could put me on a forward path.

I could, said the forest, shifting
in the wind, *but you seem more inclined
to circles and dead ends.*

That's well documented, I confessed.
But change is my wheelhouse—
maybe you can set me right.

A softer slant of light slipped
through the canopy, sharpening
the shadows of the undergrowth.

Then tell me what you know about forests,
it suggested. *Answers often come
from common ground.*

I know the single tree is separate
from the whole, I offered.

Is it?

Certainly, I said. Remove one tree
and the forest is still the forest.

*Then cut me down, stick by stick,
to a lone pine: Am I still the forest?*

No, you've taken it too far, I said.
One tree is not a forest.

And yet I started as a single tree,
countered the forest,
shrugging its rough bark.
At what point was my essence whole?

I'll have to think about that, I said.

You think too much, said the forest,
that's your problem.
Besides, only one thought matters.

Which one, I asked,
thinking of so many.

Survival, proclaimed the forest.
That's what sets the rules
in this neck of the woods.

But what about beauty? I said.
Flowers in springtime, and what not?

Don't talk to me about springtime,
the forest rumbled. *I'd skip*
that turf war altogether if I could.

Above me dead limbs creaked.
Ascending vines of kudzu, grape,
and ivy choked every flaking trunk.

But surely you contemplate the
significance of it all, I said.
Surely it has crossed your mind
that something otherworldly
drives us, and we are more than
a collection of interlocking parts.
Surely you sense the ghost
in your own machine.

I focus on growth, said the forest,
shaking loose a shower of storm debris.
Whatever dies will feed whatever lives.
The continuity sustains me.

That's fine for you, I said,
but I'm neither forest nor tree.
My nature is to search for continuity
outside the cycle of decay.

All nature is decay, argued the forest,
whether light rises or falls.

Then maybe your catalogue
is incomplete, I suggested.
Maybe nature is empty
of whatever it is I seek.

There's nowhere else to search,
huffed the forest, its chilly breath
weaving through the brambles.
There is only the singularity of the tree,
and the multiplicity that follows.

I'm not so sure about that, I said.

Because you're rootless, chided
the forest. *You have no grip*
to hold you steady on the earth.

Then I will be unsteady, I said,
and walk whatever crooked line I can.

You won't get very far that way,
scoffed the forest.
Where you'll wind up is anybody's guess.

You're probably right, I said.
But the mystery sustains me.

In spite of the
heat we sat un
covered in the

vegetable gar
den and simmered
in the wild still

ness; she took out
her teeth to show
me how old she

was and said when
you're ninety you
forget things but

you still know more
than you need to.

Ten Haiku About
the Limitations of the
Heart, with One Missing

The mirror reflects
the face that reflects the world
that holds the mirror.

Light brightens any
space, but that's illusion; there
are still bills to pay.

We watch for someone
to appear, but the heart has
four clouded windows.

Every storm kills some
thing, but keep smiling: nothing
distracts like rainbows.

Dance and the heart will
thaw; thaw and the heart will dance.
But mind the music.

The empty street and
the crowded street are the same:
strangers remain strange.

Language is the mask
concealing our uneven
heartbeats from the world.

In pure wilderness
the only clear path is the
one right behind you.

So in the smallest
of rooms, which is to say the
heart, we rest at last.

Extend a cane, angled
into a clear pool and
see how the water lies.

A green streetlamp
casts a reddish shadow
on the snow.

Horizon lines waver
in summer heat, liquid
as light.

A ghost appears,
then vanishes,
in the corner of an eye.

Little is what or where
it claims to be.

Nothing is honest,
save the ordinary
question mark,
a curve in space amid
a world
of straight deceptions,

a symbol severed from
its lower self,
a clear sign of wonder,

an endless voice with
no pretense of knowing.

But Then Face to Face   1976

I stared straight
into noon
to find direction

directly
the accommodating
sun stopped dead

and spun me for
a while
on fiery fingers

Seen enough? he asked

And all I could say
was
      yes

What I should know by now is a mystery.
Most of what I've learned has puddled
back into darkness. In the larger scheme
I'm flypaper in the Arctic, the extended

warranty, picture-in-picture, whatever
useless thing we tack on afterwards.
I breathe and move and hold together
because my smallest building blocks

serve vital functions I could never name,
which is science giving way to belief.
My capillaries toil without encouragement,
my membranes manage jobs beyond my

comprehension, my neurons fire, if only
as an article of faith. My wisdom teeth
continue to lie low. My father kept
secrets in his spinal fluid and the doctors

tapped him like an old-growth maple,
week after week, fifty times before the
surgery. But no answers surfaced in
their Magic 8-Ball. He died badly.

My mother, too, for that matter,
her leg bones so brittle they snapped
when she stood. Sixty pounds at the
end. My own ticket remains uncertain,

a *finity* that has not let me *in*. What I
do know by now is a disappointment.
My brain can barely think itself whole.
Cells uncouple daily. Still, breakage

has its upside. The gramophone needle
skips backward, and we think, *déjà vu*.
The oil stain by the curb recalls the
four bright colors of childhood.

Pain becomes the old dog in the yard,
snarling but half-toothless. Superstition
saves us from our darkest thoughts,
as blessings, we imagine, bloom in

multiples of three. So what if the shattered
glass loses water? On the slick sidewalk
every dangerous shard sparkles, every
spilled drop evaporates toward home.

When the Teacher Is Ready, the Student Will Appear

2015

At the big university
there's a
No Trespassing sign
on the School
of World Studies.

Nearby, mathematicians
don't notice;
they're busy
summing up the problem.

Across campus
among the philosophers
Socrates
goes on screaming

*Know thyself, you
stupid sons of bitches!*

but the sound
doesn't carry
quite far enough.

a lone weed
leans
informally
against the
wind's
imagination

yielding up
its will
to
circumstance

this is
the best side
of
perfection

real balance
needs
an accidental
look

Ophelia

It should be noted, just for the
record, that when Ophelia last said
Lord, we know what we are, she did

not yet know about the Heisenberg
Uncertainty Principle, nor the fact
that her own written potential

was a pretty short line of motion
running up the angle of a willow
and a brook. For all practical

purposes it was here, at the angle's
open end, that she fulfilled the
last of her particulars and fell

into the old unwritten flow; and
any meantime tunes that may have
lined the course of her demise were

nothing more than peripheral after-
thoughts, dissipating nonchalantly
toward the center of the sea.

When motion
from a
great height
falls
into the tangible
as windslide
passing into
landslide
does,
a kind of
losing balance
is maintained
along
the line
of its
translation.
The slope
takes on a
different
slant
while wind
disperses
in the
jackpine groves.

A Note to My Daughters, Far Away

The heat of the afternoon has eased into
the gray haze of evening; the oak tree, with
its broad city of leaves, stands still as the
earth beneath it. Time slows, as it always
does for the solitary watcher. Were I not here,
time might falter altogether. As it is, my faint
shadow in the fading light will soon be gone.

O my daughters: for you I wish nothing
too steep, too far, too difficult to hold.

Given sad choices, I would wish you doubt
before I would wish you pain. I would wish
you pain before I would wish you loneliness.
I would never wish you fear—that inmost cave
where souls lose sight of everything. I've
wandered there for more eternities than I
can say, yet still believe there is a lighted
pathway back. Longing is unavoidable,
so live with it as best you can. Let it be
an ally, the hunger that propels the hunt.

In every case, maintain a celebration.
Remember some bright pool, some dance of
light through leaves, some spread of color from
a sinking sun. The dark descends only to
remind us: existence was a long shot at best, but
luck was with us. Let all complaints be feathers.

Forget stars. The universe is a dark place—
and getting darker, physics tells us,
as the emptiness expands.
That's why we tell stories.
Hokum offers hope, and we fall for it,
in spite of the odds. Even
with the sidewalk buckling beneath our feet,
we break out the Sunday best
and hustle along to whatever meeting
we can't be late for.

There's always fear enough to go around,
though the why of it depends on what
corner you've backed yourself into, what
catastrophe you've crawled your way out of.
Flaws in the heart, that's all it comes down to;
the ceaseless beating.

We try to navigate the darkness
but vision dissipates,
the same as if we'd stared into the sun.
Maybe there's a deer crossing the road,
maybe a fallen tree, but the fog thickens,
and we can't slow down. Things happen.

Questions as to what we're doing here
seem natural at first, maybe even helpful,
as we stumble our way into the jungle,
the desert, the ice-choked sea.
Are we alone in all this? we ask.
But the mystery only conjures up
a waterfall of dubious replies,
some of which make monsters out of fools—
the suicide bomber, say, or the raging gunman;
the racist, the prophet, the betrayed lover
barreling past some point of no return—
all of them haunted
by one hooded specter or another.
No wonder we glance over our shoulders

in strange neighborhoods.
At times it seems like
something doesn't want us here.

But that's not so.
Whatever half-baked notion
launched us into light, we're here
because the universe made room,
and whether you believe in
magic gardens or dinosaurs,
and whether we arrived
at the end of a short work week or
after fourteen billion years of simmering,
nothing crosses that threshold
without belonging.

And unlike stone
we know we're here.

We also know
what temporary means.

The universe knows it too,
knows infinity is an overstatement
from the math department, eternity
a gross exaggeration from the terrified.
The endgame stops abruptly at the grave,
and the grave is universal.
Each star is destined to flame out,
each atom destined to break down.
The only difference between us
and everything
is one of scale.

The meantime: that's our common ground.

We're more than just some
groaning hulk of meat roaming the planet.
We're the mirror, set here to reflect.

We're part of the show, part of the audience,
but also the critic waiting in the wings,
evaluating what goes on.
Maybe we hate that part of the job,
excavating old bones
to verify history's worst nightmares,
all the killings and the rest of it.

But even at our worst
we're no more flawed than anything else.
Ask the nearest black hole
how hard it is not to destroy;
ask the nearest supernova.
A stray comet could wipe us out with no regrets,
so stealing that box of pencils from the storeroom
might not be as damning as you thought.
Perspective: that's one thing we can offer.

Purpose is another, as we delve into the dark.
Longing, too, expansive as an open sky;
and meaning, in our opposition
to the cold dead certainties of stone.

The blue ball loops along the galaxy floor
while we look forward and back, inside and out,
noting every blip in the cosmos—
the faint emissions from the nebulae,
the faint vibrations in the spider's web.
We were born to perceive,
and perception puts existence on the map.
For the time being, at least;
no matter how secure the prison,
time has a way of running out.

But that's okay.
So what if your life has been
a slow climb up a dunghill—get over it.
If you lack direction, find the horizon.
If you lack a reason, imagine tomorrow.
If you lack imagination, retire to the attic

and rummage through the remnants
of your childhood.
In any case, let logic run the carousel.
Sure, a universe is just one turn,
but notice the long curve ahead.
From the atom to the solar system,
we're caught up in circles; circles everywhere.
What more reassurance do we need?

Once long ago, when the earth was rounder
than it is today and spun like a marble on the
kitchen floor of time, there lived two small
creatures of existence: one was named Being,
the other was Not. And one fine spring morning
when the sun was shining and the breeze was
cool, and everything was just about as real as it
had ever been, Being and Not sat down together
as friends on a piece of green clover and began
to talk. And they talked as friends often do, about
this and that and nothing in particular; and as the
dew melted and their conversation came to an
end, they decided to divide up all the *am*s and
*is*es of the world and go on along their separate
ways. They took turns choosing, and both of
them picked the things they wanted most. Being
got the trees, the clouds, the birds, the wind;
she got color, and song, and the simpler portions
of imagination; she got rivers, and mountains,
and light from the moon; and she was happy.
But no happier than Not, who also got all the
things he'd ever wanted—for he got unicorns,
and dragons, and all the elves and trolls and
pixies, whom he loved; he got the very highest,
farthest, deepest portions of imagination; he
got wishes, and dreams, and ghosts, and magic.
And before long everything that ever was
belonged to Being or to Not—except for one
last thing. It was a small thing, but it was
something they both wanted. So they decided
to flip a coin: heads, it went to Being; tails, it
went to Not. It came up heads. And here we are.

TODAY'S LESSONS IN THE ANIMAL KINGDOM

the space we know is finite
wings are more for consolation
than escape
      even in flight
      a bird is tethered

a winter portrait of
fifty black vultures in a
sycamore tree
moves no one
      but a portrait of destruction
      fires the mind

hunters flush a pheasant from
the field and bring it down:
feelings vary by circumstance
      joy for the hungry
      sorrow for the empathetic

pleasure for the damaged
or inadequate
something else for the rest
      meaning ought to
      fit in somewhere

preserve the single bird
blasted from the sky
open a place in memory for
whatever abstract notion
captures the fall

Hummingbird and Hawk

What surprises me most about
hummingbirds is their viciousness.
We've hung feeders on the back of
the house, and I've watched from the
kitchen window, just inches away:
oil-slick greens and blues, iridescent
in the sun; ruby throats on some.
A dozen or more might swarm the
red glass jars, squabbling over the
false flower's fake nectar. They'll
drain a quart of sugar water in a day.

A fragile, delicate bird—the beak
a slender thorn, the body a
mere afterthought of creation. The
smallest can weigh less than a penny.

But their recklessness of attack,
even when food is plentiful, suggests
an inborn state of panic, a lack of
judgment, an incomplete understanding
of what a summer day might bring.

Or maybe I'm the one
who doesn't understand.

Sometimes they rest on the yellow
rim of the feeder's base, appearing
ordinary, drab as a dwarf sparrow.

Flight is their comfort zone, wings
fanning faster than the eye can see,
seventy beats per second. All day long
they fight, bulleting through the yard,
beak to tail, banking left and right, each the
interloper to the other's hunger and desire.

Nearby, our red-tailed hawk sits
solitary and calm on the top rail at

the front end of the pasture. He often
perches close to the horses—their
clumsy hooves will sometimes flush
out prey, and he'll swoop deftly to the
ground for a field mouse no bigger
than a hummingbird. He takes no
notice of the hummingbirds themselves,
those fidgety impersonators that lack a
raptor's knack for ripping flesh from bone.

Hawk: even the word lodges like a
hatchet in green wood. Sometimes he
rides the high thermals, seeing everything.

He once allowed me to approach,
holding my stare until he lost interest.
When I crowded too close, just five
steps away, he noted my impertinence
by gliding a few rails farther down the
line, more dismissive than fearful. No
doubt he's seen what humans can do, but
has nevertheless pegged me as a weakling—
grounded, no stealth at all, no speed,
no patience, my talons flimsy and dull.

Neither bird, I suspect, shares my
fondness for rain on rusted tin, sees
faces in the clouds, builds a logical
argument, leaves a proper tip. The hawk
cries out its presence across the brambled
fields, the hummingbird chirps petty
objections. Neither bird has a song.

Maybe that's our common ground.

The hawk dwells mostly in stillness,
in ownership. The hummingbird
flits, a timid trespasser in the hostile
air, its wild heart buzzing.

And yet they're both birds, which means
that somewhere in the misty backstory
of life, they shared a common ancestor,
some bird-like thing that laid a clutch of
eggs of unequal size, unequal possibility,
and the great divergence began.

Meanwhile, I walk between the two,
imagining kinship with both
hummingbird and hawk, part of me
believing the nectar-filled world has
tumbled toward a terrifying end,
part of me believing it never will.

When the eagle drops the turtle
from a great height,
it knows what it's doing.
That's how it makes a living.
The turtle will land hard,
preferably on rocks, and split apart,
allowing easy access to the meat.

But what does the turtle
make of it all?
Falling from the sky
outstrips its understanding.
As far as any turtle knows,
gravity is harmless,
a slow pull toward lethargy,
a simple means of staying put.
Shell-shattering force
is a mystery for the afterlife,
a puzzle inherited by blood,
a secret text hidden among the
picked-over remains of the fallen.

In that moment of release
does the turtle think it's free
to get on with its life?
Is it pleased by the weightless
downward rush, relieved
to have slipped the grip
of whatever it was
that snatched it up
from its sunny slant of stone
on the warm bank beside the water?
Is the last thing it feels
a surge of joy
as it accelerates headlong
toward what it has known only
as the safety of its home?

And what if it somehow lives,
landing lightly on a cushion

of thick brush, or slicing edgewise
back into a mossy pond?
What facts of the miraculous
can it pass along to others
of its kind when there are no
others of its kind? Experience
speaks a language all its own.
Survivors are both blessed and
cursed, and have to live alone
with what they know.

Who among the ordinary could
believe in talons from the sky,
the terrifying rapture of being
taken up, the ecstasy of flight,
the freedom of the great fall,
the shock of reuniting
with the rising earth?
Who among the innocent
could comprehend the
darkness of the turtle's dream,
the one that now
casts its shadow over
all remaining moments in the sun?

.

The crow knows only
one approach:
Avoid what watches.

The crow knows
a straw hat on a cross
is no harbinger
and sits upon the
scarecrow's raveled sleeve.

The crow knows enough
to fear the airport,
homeland of the gods.

The crow knows black
is the brightest color.

The crow knows there is no
separation between the days.

The crow knows birdsong
is useless.

The crow knows
what it means to say.

The crow knows the bounty
that rises after the storm.

The crow knows what
to leave behind,
what to take away.

Crow Song

The mockingbird
sat quiet
which was its way
of doing mountain.

But no one
tossed a crumb
his way
or marveled
in the least
at his perception.

Disgusted,
he laid fault
with the high crags;
and straining
his voice uphill,
he swore
at the barrenness
of perfection,
at his talent
left speechless
in the trees.

Sarah, Unbroken

My wife, Dawn, a natural caretaker, found
a car-struck fawn by the roadside and brought
it home, a doubtful rescue from the start.
She laid it in a stall bedded with fresh sawdust
and set food and water within its reach.

It never drank or fed. Our soft voices were
no balm for its broken back, and nothing ever
calmed its panic into rest. Nevertheless,
we named her, that ancient human habit so
prominent among our weaknesses.

If need is great, some animals surrender to a
soothing touch, regardless of what instinct
has to say. But others don't, and this one
clung to fear as if it were her only hope.
She died before the week was out, the only

ending possible, and we grieved as if we had
an owner's right. Maybe that was empathy,
or maybe just the same old hubris, left over
from those first free days in Eden, when naming
was the only means we had to stake a claim.

But either way, she was never less than wild, and
nothing about her was ever really ours except
her name, that artificial thread of kinship and
belonging, an illusion strung between ourselves
and the damage we bring daily to the world.

The horses need more room to run,
so I'm pulling fence posts that divide
the larger field. It's late July, heat
shimmers from the yellow dirt, and

I pace myself, digging a while,
sorting old boards, digging again.
I guess correctly as I turn the knotted
planks, expecting black widows

before finding them. We're infested
here. I step with purpose on the
largest one, but when I lift my
boot, she's gone. I pick my shovel

up again. The job takes longer than
I thought it would, as most jobs do.
Each inch is earned, so tight and
sure the stonelike grip of earth. The

horses watch my progress from a
farther field, flinching against deer
flies, patient in the sun. The dog
watches from the porch, too wise

to leave the shade. Were I his equal,
I'd have no posts to pull, no tools to
work the reclaimed land. I'd hold
no obligation here, feel no owner's

urge to measure and confine. As it
is, I'm tethered to these few acres,
a minor stop on Lee's retreat toward
Appomattox. Spent bullets from the

war undercoat the territory, but true
history carves a broader trail. Here's
what solid ground has taught me:
there is no solid ground. Each

fence row is a fluid thing, no matter
how deep the posts are set. The
straight line I etched across the field
last year broke ranks in early spring.

The soil loosened and shifted, erasing
all my efforts at precision and control,
then hardened into place again.
That's natural enough. The earth

breathes upheaval, making and un-
making mountains with a shrug.
Around here weeds and vines handle
the small stuff, dismantling whatever

board and brickwork we devise.
The dog offers a lethargic yawn, and
I suspect he's right. Our deeds are
made of paper; the rest is made of clay.

The old routines
          soon disappear.

Today my wife
          milked a dead cow
          to save its newborn calf,
a white bull tangled
in ropy afterbirth.

She scissored the cold cord
          and hauled the bloody
          breathing mess
down the hillside to the barn,
          warmed it with a blanket.
          By afternoon it
stood steady on its own.

But later in the same field,
          as she worked the
          unbroken stallion
          on a training line,
three jack burrows, stern
watchdogs of the cattle herd,
          crested the hill
                    and charged.

The spooked stallion whirled
                    and trampled her,
          then dragged her down
          the rocky slope.
A cracked sternum and more.

          As usual, she
shrugged it off,
content to hold her balance
between misfortune
          and sheer grace.

In some worlds
the inexplicable always
        marries the inevitable,
                and we dance
like relatives from
        out of town,
            reeking of mothballs,
devouring
        the white cake afterwards.

Understanding is a threshold
to be broken twice: the wrong
idea, followed by the right.

Wrong is often more agreeable.

When I first heard the word,
I felt confusion, then delight:
melancholy on a child's blank slate
carries no darkness.
Instead, a form impossible for the
wise to see assembles itself
in the unworldly mind.

I pictured a dog,
part melon, part collie.
A shiny green body,
four legs of twining vines,
a wagging stem of a tail,
a leafy tongue lolling
from a mouth that smiled.
My melancholy dog was happy.

And why not?
Nothing in an untried world
requires a somber mood.
Innocence is an empty state,
a yardstick by which
we measure loss,
so I was busy cataloging data:
water was wet, rocks were hard,
heat was hot, pain was painful.
Being new here was a full-time job.

I knew by then what horses were.
Sometimes they carried cowboys
across the grassy plain.
Sometimes they hauled
storybook gods across the sky.

Only later would I sort the differences,
distinguish mind from body,
separate the mythic from the real.

After breathing, misinformation
is the first high hurdle of childhood.

After breathing, misinformation
is the first safe haven of childhood.

But when our fun with Dick and Jane
is done, after we've seen Spot run,
disillusionment dog-ears every page.
Horseflies turn out not to be the
fairyland wonder we first thought.
They're bloodsuckers,
always on the attack.

On the educated side of life,
discoveries are rare.
I find there's not much meat on a
chicken wing, and when a little kid
yells, *Look at me, I'm a monkey!*
the broken arm comes next.

Crestfallen is our loveliest word
for disappointment.

For twelve years I've lived with
horses that do not fly. My wife
repairs the ones in need, and so
I've learned of all the fatal options:
torn tendons, colic, bloody abscesses,
laminitis, ataxia, infectious anemia,
West Nile virus, acidosis, protozoal
myeloencephalitis, the strangles,
perforated coffin bones, brain fever,
broken vertebrae, Cushing's
Syndrome, and the inability to sweat.

We had an Irish Sport Horse that
ran a splintered fence board through
its skull. Fragile in so many ways.

But sometimes indestructible.
When a friend's horse got hit
by a truck on the highway,
my wife plunged her arm
inside its open chest and gripped
the torn artery shut until
the vet arrived. That horse survived.

It's all a mystery.
We've put down strong spirits
that foundered for no clear reason,
and mad spirits, and gentle spirits.
The best, called Beau, is
buried in our yard between a
thriving birch and a dying magnolia.

Now, as the world shrinks with age,
we're scaling back
and giving up the farm. No more
rumbling stutter of hoofbeats
across dusty ground at feeding time,
or the sharp swish of a tail in the
smoldering stillness of a summer sun.

Our heroes once were cast as
bold equestrians in bronze or stone.
Today the horse stumbles,
obsolete as the gods themselves,
replaced by tractors on the farm,
cars on the byways;
reduced to lawn ornaments
or showpieces for games
the rich still play. Bred for speed
and thus unnaturally frail,
the finest stallion can snap a leg bone
before three-quarters of a mile.

The horse's day is done.
And yet we've found no substitute
in our mythology. No one sculpts
Churchill on a Volkswagen,
Eisenhower grinning from his golf cart,
seven-iron in hand. No one chisels
Gandhi riding the roller coaster or
Mother Theresa skimming the waves
on a jet ski, a surge of horsepower
keeping her afloat.

Our statuary has shriveled into
life-sized likenesses
of unassuming souls at ease in
business suits, pausing on a
morning's walk, often with a cane.
No sword held high, no armored
breastplate, no rearing steed.
At most, a pensive look ahead.

On the placid lawn outside
the administration building,
a bronze man sits posed
on a park bench, resting, as if
metal fatigue has already set in,
as if he's tired of celebrating
his own mild heroism, wearied
by the glory of who he was.

Our very dreams, it seems,
have been diminished by the exit
of the horse, and I'm awash in
what the ancients called *black bile,*
dark product of the gall bladder,
marked by foul humors and
a lengthening of depressive dread.

The word they coined for such a state,
I since have learned, is *melancholy.*

Considering the Origins of Mysticism
on a Visit to Texas

The bats beneath Congress Avenue Bridge
        hang motionless in sallow light.

        Come sundown, when distinctions
blur for the dilating eye,
they drop and swoop, then
        climb the hungry spiral of departure,

up over the guardrails and higher,
a chaos of need channeling off
                into the nourishing winds.

A sign on the northern bank says
                Never Handle Grounded Bats,
a late commandment
        we are not inclined to quibble with.

We know these aren't the shrill grackle
or the comical catbird.
        We know there are teeth involved.
        Whatever chip rests
                on whatever shoulder
we'll save our doubts for other days.

On the southern approach a sculpture
of a giant bat bears witness,
        pays tribute
        in sharp curves and black angles.
Passersby stare in wonder at the plaque
        and read all they need to know about
civic pride and twilight spectacle.
Still, few return at nightfall.

We like our bats beneath the bridge,
        not rising up around us
                like a rapture of dark angels,
not thickening the air with shrieks
                and beating wings.

But that's not altogether true.

Some do come back, again and again,
for that chilly glimpse
of something large enough to fear,
a dark river of sinew and bone snaking
heavenward through the faltering sky.

It's love of mystery that lures us
through the first unsteady steps
of our undoing,
strands us squarely in the nightmare's path,
where any swarm of
bloodsuckers may or may not
choose to pass us by.

Such brushes feed the slumping heart.

Go ask the tramp panhandling on the span.
His smile is genuine as he works
the watching crowd.
He understands the present state,
knows that if we have to face a thing
each day, we have to learn to love it.

Fishing

Everyone has lines to drop in somewhere.
Most folks take to rivers, where their
progress is a clean, apparent thing: where

the casting angle pulls down through the
fast, clear surface of the shallows and
sets the lure in open spin against the run.

From there it's easy to anticipate the
strike, to watch the speckled trout rise
from the speckled sand and wind around

the current to the lure, angling for the
line, then breaking surface for the impact
and the play.

                    But clarity in shallows
gives no insight into depths. I'd rather
plumb my line, and let it settle in the

still brown blend of pond and bottom,
deep down in silt, and fish for things
I have no chance of seeing.

Progress
might be too optimistic a word
for what we're making.

When wilderness was status quo,
grim pilgrims stood their ground.

We're soft as rain-soaked grass.
We spend our lives in track shoes,
shifting on hot pavement,
cold pavement, buckled pavement.
We stroll the malls.
Between vacations we
calibrate machines to put up walls
between nature
and our well-dressed selves.

But time disrupts even as it levels,
and I'm the outlier
on the ragged edge, settled in
against the rough back of the woods.

I hammer fence boards,
hack away at stumps, stack hay
in storage sheds. I rake the stalls
and haul manure to the fields.

But something watches from
a hidden perch. Cougars
have marked our woodlands,
our pastures, as their own.
A young one crossed our road at dusk:
the tail long, the body sleek and low.
At night we hear the squalls,
like an infant crying to be fed.

The lame horse in the near paddock
spooks at nightfall, frantic for the barn.
The dogs bark at what's unseen.
Everything that lives here qualifies as
prey, even the well-educated, and
somewhere in that common blackness
is a thing that can't be reasoned with.
It's ready, should the stumble come.

We still walk out on moonless nights
for necessary chores, a tuned ear
turned always toward the brush.
I keep a pitchfork by the riding ring
and scan the trees for eyes.

Tonight I'm traveling, safe among
strangers, cruising the blank sky
at an altitude no animal could dream.

Even this is wilderness,
and nature's lesson is the same:
all flights are temporary.
We might delay, delay,
and then delay again,
but the cat is down there waiting,
its need growing
with each passing winter's day.

On U.S. 220 coming
down the rock hills
between Roanoke and

Martinsville, an old
half-breed beagle and I
second-guessed each

other three times running
on what ought to be
the best move to make.

After that he just gave
up and braced himself;
and I can't say, but I

think he was thinking,
Why the hell aren't you
smarter than a dog?

Where the gravel easement
forks away toward other homes
beyond our land,
an old woman in a rusted truck
pulled up beside me
and rolled her window down.
I thought she might be lost.

Your dog kilt my cat, she said,
her voice level as water.

I told her she was wrong.
Our yard was fenced.
The yellow lab was gentle, frail,
and rarely left the porch.
He lived with four cats of his own.
Moreover, cancer had removed
a portion of his jaw
and left him with no bite.

He kilt my cat, she said,
her truth unassailable.
My daughter say she saw it all.

I spoke about the stray I'd seen
scavenging the neighborhood,
but she dismissed my theory
with a snorted breath.

He kilt my cat, she said again.
But I don't care.

I argued still, while she just
scowled and shook her head.

I told you I don't care, she said.
A week ago my
great-granddaughter died.
I got no extra room to mourn.

I told her I was sorry for her loss.

It just a cat, she said,
and drove on up the lane.

FLESH EATERS ON PARADE

The Night before the Operation

Procedure unfolds
like a Swiss Army scalpel.
He signs his name eleven times
for a cloth bracelet,
pisses in a paper cup.
A dry nurse questions him
by clipboard: all his answers
are *no*.
She plans an enema tonight.

He reflects on all the broccoli
and carrots he never ate,
wishes his wife hadn't rear-ended
his anesthesiologist's Porsche.

The doctor drops by
to field his worries while
a young woman draws his blood.
Breathing rattles in the hall.

Near midnight, propped up
and drugged, he watches
sleep cloud the mirror,
thinks only
if he shoots his own
reflection in the glass,
bullet will always meet bullet.

The parents of the dead boys
look for justice
like old men look for buses
in the snow. Their faces
crack with weathering.

The young judge, cool
as tennis on the lawn,
wipes his glasses clean and
reads his reason to the Court:
death obligates
an exercise of Law.

The reporter glances through
his notes, then slips out
to find a phone.

But the boy who
went cold at the roller rink
leans into the counsel table
and takes in the sentence
with no look at all.
He understands destruction.
He knows emotions are
useless things, the twistings
of a cat dropped
wrongways down a well,
the havoc of two boys laughing.

A Ten-Year-Old Boy Discovering
the Certainty of Descent

1982

He knew the season well enough
to know the spring.
He knew there would be tadpoles
feeding in the water moss,
crawfish curled under
chunks of slate, and minnows,
quick without reason,
stranded side-stream
since the runoff dried.

But this day
it was the cliff he took to,
climbed without thinking,
found chinks
and temporary toeholds in;
and there he stuck,
forty feet up the rock face,
a weed out of season,
frantic to take root.

Like Jesus, what I need is a place to
come back from. Not dead, nothing mystical.
Religion is okay for starters, but
it's mostly an acknowledgments page, that
up-front tip of the hat to what is. I
need a firmer perch along the timeline.
Something optimistic: a ballpark in
the major leagues, with sticky armrests and
a bad angle on the sun. When a line
drive drills the seat beside me, suddenly
I'm more than I was, awake to blue-sky
risks—a good thing to be in small doses.

We all long for that mysterious rush,
the shiver of knowing what specter just
passed by, how lucky we have been. The spun
coin lands heads or tails, but we want both, our
lives on edge. The comic frown, the tragic
laugh. No easy truths. Events have curbed our
childish faith in circuses or church, and
now we're skeptics of the rituals we
loved. Water into wine, wine into blood,
bread into body, body into god.
Infinities of clowns climbing from the
toy car. Death-defying leaps in either
venue. Go right ahead, if you think you
can: scale that altar to the highest wire.
We're each allowed one fatal mistake. From
flesh and blood to *dead and buried*. We know
the short, swift hop from *animal* to *meat*.

Among my faults: I see no difference
between *ghost* and *apparition*. I choose
the write-in candidate. I contemplate
the sound of three hands clapping. I'm not that
worried about asbestos. Sometimes I
almost repeat myself. I see no difference
between *ghost* and *history*. If we had
to start from scratch, I could not invent glass,

or glue, or plastic. I could not devise
color film for my camera. The concept
of veneer would not occur to me. While
my chums chiseled arrowheads, I would sketch
the rudiments of parliamentary
procedure. I would comment wryly on
our predicament without solving it.
I would arrange people in rows. I would
shake hands. I would offer condolences.

On the plus side, I tend to recycle.
I wait my turn, often without success.
I smile politely. When put on hold, I
know enough to be reminded of my life.

The future may speak volumes even now,
but we don't know the tongue. A buffalo
born white. A timely flush in spades. A
bad dream dissipating like morning mist.
The Hanged Man crossing The Fool. All useless
clues, for the most part, like highway signs in
Braille. Still, something fantastic, or at least
preliminary, lies just ahead, we
know it. *The World* is our collective term
for *traffic jams,* but things untangle in
the end. Might as well hope. Maybe there's a
green light afterwards, a cure for what ails
you, a woman who rides wild horses, a
voice to tell you secrets of the trade. Or
maybe you'll buy a sad house in winter,
not knowing every spring the yard erupts
in bright perennials. It's possible.

But what do I know? Mostly what I do
is wait for the mail, water the dogs, or
worry about my internal organs.
I'm adrift in old guesswork. If it weren't
for books, I wouldn't know I had any
thing but a heart, hung slightly off-center

in an open cage amid a snarled mass
of tubing. The beatings go on daily.

In the beginning was the *Word*, making
language fundamental. What's DNA
but yesterday's dictation, a raw text
ready to be transcribed. We're all rough draft
material, though they never spelled
that out in Sunday School. I heard it on
the radio one night, idling at a
dark crossroad, waiting for the light to change.
Maybe I didn't wait quite long enough.
Maybe that was my mistake.

At the Museum of Natural History
the church group from Winosha
smiles at everything.

There are no dinosaurs
where they come from.

Summer mornings, mowers
wake them, natural as bees.
Wives wear bathrobes on the porch,
the men keep socks in folded pairs.

Workmen in another block
hammer a house together,
call jokes across a leveled lot.

Tyrannosaurus Rex looks
smaller than they'd hoped,
his grin less menacing.
They move on to the penguin case,
discussing sandwiches.

The children stay behind
to watch the bones.

You've been brought here to visit and
this is how it ends: you wake before
the house, before the birds, and go out
into your great-grandfather's yard for
oranges. In the tall grass near the shed
your breathing brings the chickens out.
They shadow you, expecting feed. You
find an orange, but it's old, sticky on
one side. You slip your thumb beneath
the peel and pull: ants pour across your
fingers. This is not what you want. You
hear a rustle in the trees and look up at
the branch, but you're too late, it's gone,
the bird, the green chameleon. Instead
you see oranges, yellow oranges,
and you think, *This is what I want*. You
put your foot against the trunk and
start to climb, but the bark surprises
you, draws blood. You try again, hug
the tree more gently, give weight to
your hands, but thorns are everywhere,
you can't avoid them, and halfway up
your palms begin to bleed. The branches
cluster tighter as you climb, barbs snag
your arms and chest, a small spike
stabs your head, your knee, but you
don't stop, you're determined, and you
move out on a limb, still climbing toward
a good one, toward one just ready to drop.

What we can't say is everywhere.

This morning while the younger stallion
rolls in dust to coat himself
against the flies, I pull thistles from the
barbed-wire stretch behind the pond.

The purple blooms look soft
and bright as childhood
but sting as deeply as the stalks.

Nothing friendly grows in fence rows.

I duck with care through the
spotted shade of the Osage orange—
hedge apple, we call it here—
its branches lined with slender spikes.

By afternoon I've moved on to the
tight weave of buckthorn and briar
that curves across the floodplain of
the low front field.
Every fencepost leans rotten
against the slack of unstrung wire.
I bake beneath the glare of a clear sky,
my arms bloody with reprimands.

Back at the sheet-metal barn
a small frog clings to a window pane.
A stork, the first I've ever seen,
passes purposefully overhead.

The house waits quietly, though
five blue-backed baby barn swallows
clamor from a nest above the porch.
The sun goes silver behind its usual hill.
Moments gather, possibly without end.

Still, what we can't say is everywhere.

Dark is a narrow easement.
Dawn is a word I love.
Sometimes storms wash through
the valley, and the cold stream strays
across the road. But not today.

I scrape my boots clean with a goat bone
left over from the dogs' night out
and think which portions
of the widening earth
I'll try to move tomorrow.

The crush at Union Station had no
meaning, but it shoved her hard.
She shrugged it off as background,
impersonal as her piece of bench.

Her two-year-old, tied loosely
to her wrist, climbed
the mismatched luggage at her feet.
A baby harnessed to her back cried out
and pitched his bottle to the floor.
She bent to fetch it,
doubling at her pregnant waist.
Her dress fit tight and raveled
from the weaker seams.
Her eyes, watery behind thick lenses;
her hair, a shock of straw.
A beauty queen made homely
by a circumstance.

Her mother, the peroxide blonde,
had come to see her off.
Don't cry now, Babe, she said.
Still young herself, though ravaged
by chain cigarettes and sun.
Complexion like sandstone.
Chipped nails, gaunt hips, bad teeth.
She lifted up the tethered boy and
told him he should always say his
prayers. *I'll drop you now,* she laughed,
and dipped him to the baggage pile,
pretending he could fall.

When the young hotshot fakes right
and blurs past you to the basket,
suppress the reflex of denial.
It makes no difference if last year

you might have stopped him, planting
a sure foot inside the lane to draw the
charge. It's a new season, the brain
lies half awake to old motions, cold

muscles can't remember what they knew.
Even your wife suspects. She sees you
after workouts, moving on your bones
like stilts. Quick games are for quick

players, she thinks, though what she
says is noncommittal, something about
last month's utility bills, taping fresh
plastic to the windows, the wind's been

slipping through the cracks again. . .
She's partly right: each climate carries
problems all its own. In the steaming
gym you pace yourself, adjust and

compensate for years spent thickening
like glue, holding the loose bricks
of your life together. The younger
ones don't feel it yet, don't see the

uselessness of score, don't know a
game's been won if it's been weathered.
To them you're just slow cargo in the
current, buoyant as a grinding stone.

Still, you take the ball down court
and work it to the open man. By now
you've learned there's more than
speed involved, more than the mindless

arc of ball clearing a steel rim. If
all you do is make the inbounds pass
or even-up the sides, it's enough,
it keeps you there; and in a long

stretch of game you can still pick
your moment, still catch some rising
star flatfooted with a quick pivot
and a fade-away jump. And before the

ball has even left your hands, you see
the perfect path it climbs. That moment,
hanging in the thick, hot air, you
outplay every ghost you've ever known.

A man stares too long
at the sun
then falls in love
with what he thinks
he sees.
He raves, naturally.

Listeners gather,
mistaking blindness
for insight's nearest kin.

A shred of wet cardboard
streaked with
oil and rust from a
broken-bricked alley floor

becomes

a long bright room,
a flock of doves,
a circus of acrobats
and mysterious beasts
on the edge
of a golden city.

Someone sends 'round
the collection plate.
Belief will side
with what's pretty.

Coach said
If you can't play hurt,
you can't play.
Turns out he was right.

I have friends
with broken heads
and different hearts
and all those secret,
silent ailments of the blood.

But I've learned a few things.
The universe is a war
between curves and angles.
Bugs fly toward the light
that kills them. Saturdays
aren't what they used to be.
A scattering of nails
outside a tire store
is cause for suspicion.

I try smiling, but the mirror
is a growing disappointment.

True reflection
is me at seventeen,
cornering hard
with the top down,
the wind still welcome,
the road
more slippery than I thought.

Why We Don't Look Forward
to Eternal Damnation

It's a hot night. Summer sinks
　　　under its own weight,
muggy and slow. My wife and

daughters have left town, but I'm
　　　still here, half drunk,
dizzy, in a smalltime pool hall, the

first deviation in a plenitude of
　　　years. Time has left
me smoke-dull, sluggish. The first

few racks I play like any yokel
　　　off the street, missing
the long shot, never banking in.

What I know comes back slowly,
　　　like sand settling in
water, but still it comes. I grow

accustomed to the click and roll,
　　　remember how to
think beyond the shot. Through

the screen door I see thin punks
　　　lounging on car hoods.
Dogs gather by the garbage cans,

whining toward the light. Behind
　　　me, change drops
through a metal slot: music, loud

and unfamiliar, quakes the floor.
　　　A rangy hustler with
an at-home stare glides over from

the bar to make a bet. He's seen my
　　　break, casual and
unfocused, knows the stick I'm

playing with is warped. But it's a
            hot night: the cue turns
native in my hand. Double banks

drop gently into called pockets. He
            has caught me on a
streak from ten years back, and

suddenly I'm a kid with no public
            face, parents still alive,
the future stretching longer than the

past. I clear the table twice before
            he quits. I look around.
Amber light warms the paneled walls.

Jazzmen in a corner booth wave in
            my direction. A woman,
pale and bloated, one breast spilling

from her dress, leans heavily against
            a pay phone. A fat man
exits to the men's room. Even this is

unsettling. Mistakes whirl around
            me, closing in.
Experience warns that if you have to

fall, fall fast, ahead of gravity, to keep
            control. But that's not me.
In twenty years I'll be an old man

walking through an empty house at
            night. In any given group,
I'll be the guy near the heater. When

cars creep by, my skin will crawl,
            knowing some people
kill without reason. There are no

bystanders in any neighborhood, and
no one stays innocent for
long. We all ask forbidden questions,

it's in the guidebook. So what's the
point of dreams we
can't remember? What drives the

unborn chick to break the egg, not
knowing what's outside?
How long before regret sets in? When

love gets bludgeoned out of shape,
what are the options?
Bow down forever? Say *Thanks for*

shopping here? When history puts
its final block in
place, is the best we can hope for

a sympathetic call to the family and
two plastic bags
on the nursing-home floor? No.

Every dark story is apocryphal.
There's always one
more rabbit in the hat, even for the

battered and betrayed. A million
cows stand calmly
on the hillsides, contentment dulling

their senses, not one thinking of the
slaughterhouse, but
that's not us, not anyone we know.

Pain is the overlooked ally in this
world. In the long
run, be glad of every grief you own.

Splitting Up the Record Collection

He thinks ahead to what she wants
and what he knows she'll pick.
He calculates, concedes
the dozen singles first
in hopes she'll follow
with concessions of her own.
She doesn't.
Still, there are worse strategies.

He fans the albums on the rug
and she begins.
The ones she pauses over
he sees go gladly; the rest
don't matter. She leaves him
soundtracks, comedy, and Streisand.

Standing in the doorway
with his arms full,
he finds a new liking for castoffs.
He tightens his hold
and steps out onto the porch,
surprised at how easily
he gave the best away,
and staggered by the bulk
of what they
never played between them.

Estrangement 1978

Now I am alone, said Hamlet,
speaking for us both,
and for my part
I thought of our Ophelia,
dim-eyed and dozing,
ugly with indifference.

Strangely, we had lost her
while she slept,
while gravedigger sang
between father and brother,

while night rode by
openhanded,
pretending to be friend.

One hemisforce
attacks
the other hemisforce
with the same old
sterile malice
common to its cause

  and in this rush
the balance
tilts and falls

still
something in the nature
  of a clean
galactic Will

rebounds
from the empty center
  of the losing side

  shooting fire
  through the years

and slinging light
across
the reclaimed vacuum

Real-Life Romances

Real-life romances don't
start out like television

where the hero meets some
gorgeous blonde who quickly

throws her prime-time
breasts into his face and

all he has to say is my
place or yours. In real

life she has no breasts
and the guy is sweaty and

nervous, and when they meet
all he can think of to say

is turnip glup grubnoid
and she smiles but she's

really thinking Jeez, if he
was any dumber he'd be dead

ELEGY AGAINST ELEGIES

Graduation Speech for My Daughters 2003

I.

Remember everyone you meet was once
a Chinese emperor, benevolent and wise,
revered throughout the provinces
for averting civil war.
Extend your understanding
to whatever bitter seeds you see there now.

At the dinosaur museum when you were
young, guardrails kept you from the stacks
of reconnected bones, but you lingered,
staring through sockets of hip and eye.

Your own remains are videos of makeshift
musicals and homemade puppet shows.
You flicker on, tight sprays of light,
dancing out your best routines
as graceful blizzards one electron deep.

There's always greatness
in the lives we leave behind.

II.

When I was two I ran away from home.
A trooper plucked me from the highway's
center line and told me I'd been lost
since lunch. But lost had been okay.

At seventeen, I stood in Rome beside
the graves of Keats and Shelley
and swore something to myself,
although I don't remember what.

It's hard to separate the things we know
from the things we remember.

III.

In the twentieth century God became
the senile uncle, well-meaning but
bothersome, hair growing in bristles
from his ears, good only for an occasional
five bucks on birthdays or at Christmas.

As a result, my soul
fits crookedly in my body.
This
like a note from the teacher
bothers me.

It doesn't take much to renovate religion,
so before you send your fears
to military school, consider more
creative options. If Catholicism falters,
lock a vampire in a house of mirrors.
If Zen needs refurbishing,
hang wind chimes
so the pieces never touch.
Some believe in luck.
Some believe in grace,
which is the same as luck.
Some believe in science
or in science fiction.

The chosen doctrine doesn't matter
in the end. Nature has no use
for opinion. The acorn outlives the fall,
pure and simple. A good fire
needs a hollow base and always will.
The rules are elemental, but also
unforgiving, so try to think ahead.
It isn't tough to catch a tiger by surprise;
the tough part comes just after.

IV.

As intellect blossoms, ask yourself
unnecessary questions:
Why are there no more mead halls?
Can the woods ever be trusted?
Is guilt a large room to yell in
or a wool coat on a summer day?
Does the size of hell matter?
Is eternal life
eternal life,
even if it's only a
small
scattering
of heartbeats?

V.

One day I'll end up parked at some
painted stop sign waiting for it to
turn green. That's simply how it is.
The cat meows, you drift away.
The phone rings, you don't answer it.
The eyes fail: you squint to see
whatever comes too close;
you squint to see
what wavers in the distance.

We all pay dues in many unions—
that's the cost of doing business
in the world. The toll mounts,
and one by one we misplace
every graveside promise ever made.
Maybe no oath is worth breaking;
but there's no guardrail
against forgetting.

VI.

In the meantime, hold on to
what you know.
Start with a bright speck—
no, more than a speck,
a pebble, say, a bright pebble.
Now look at it against the horizon.
That's all, just look at it.

Day is almost over, the air
is dusty with too much afternoon.
An oak tree stands at
the base of the driveway.
Light still fills the neighborhood.
Every sound is a laugh.

On Thinking There Are Too Many 1977
Ways to Start a Poem about Death

Lola has her dancing dress on.
However.

We get the word some howling icon died,
but that's not stuff to slow us down.
Sure, some of us brushed past him,
time to time, but we never sat on his
apartment stairs drinking until 4 a.m.,
or heard him brag about his kids,
or saw him shred a lampshade with a
Guatemalan bullwhip, three quick strikes
that made the room go dark. That part
was played by Omar, who once hit a
dried frog dead center to beat me in
a blowgun tournament in Tyler Fleeson's
dining room. So when I hear that Omar,
too, is gone, I'm stopped.

For the most part we keep uneasiness
behind us. It pushes our sails so we can
move. The deck seems calm. Even at
funerals: the hand above the grave
serves ritual only. What dirt we sprinkle
there won't cover any ground except
our own. The hillside is littered with
handiwork, both ancient and fresh.
But we've left the age of picturesque
gravediggers, weathered sea-dogs with
their shirtsleeves rolled, leaning
patiently against long-handled shovels.
Now a man with a backhoe waits at the
mortuary garage. He'll scoop the hole
shut without daintiness. It's what we
want, after all—efficiency unslowed
by love's superstitions. Ritual is
useless except in turning us away.

Ritual is what we do best.

The cockatiels in my family room make
sharp unspellable noises like that
moment in *Psycho* when the shower
curtain gets jerked aside and the
butcher knife poses for the camera,
pausing for that eternal second before
finally striking down. An image of
Aristotelian perfection—the corrupted
naked beauty we can never save.

And Hitchcock, sly bastard, puts us
in the shower, too; feeds our voyeurism
with meaningless glimpses until there's
no escape. The consequence:
a lifetime in which to fear strange music;
a new mistrust of shadows
wavering behind transparent walls.
We know from that point on which
way our blood will circle down the drain.
We know there is no limit to the waste.

for Omar Castaneda

Rose Hill is too lumpy for the dead
to line up neatly with their neighbors.

Each swell plots off a new design,
each trough divides the stones in clusters,
parcels the land like half-played games
of chess. Rain, when it comes,
fills the chiseled words, spills down
the granite sides and seeps away.

But no name drains to dryness.
There is always some small remnant
hanging back—the damp of surface tension
clinging to its place, not following the flow.

This last remain will only give to air,
evaporate in heat beyond its form, and
disappear from place without a motion.

When the old man from the freight yards
climbs his shortcut home, he never
stops to read the markers of his friends.
They're jealous now, he thinks.

Once over the rock wall he celebrates;
dances down toward the highway
like an escaping corpse,
only one suit of clothes to his name,
and nothing in his pockets but momentum.

Still Life with Strings:
      a Disassembled Sonnet

My father has no words.
He knows as much, and
tells me when I call.
I wait while he collects
his fragments into shapes,
but it's no use: sand
pours through every net
he holds. We laugh it
off—that's one connection
left—and then I talk
about whatever's close
at hand. The fence out
back, a neighbor's health,
the plumbing, or the
weather, or the pets.
A year from now he'll be
the same curved husk
his mother was, a purpled
sack of bones. His stare
will soften, shifting
evenly from face to chair
to wall. He'll wait like
that, and I will stand
beside his bed, useless.
I'll touch his shoulder,
say some common thing.

Around the corner from the funeral home
I'm relieved to see something solid:
a beat-up Pontiac outside a liquor store,
dust thick on the hubcaps. I can guess
the farm these boys have come from.
All morning they've shoveled feed corn
from the back of a truck, filling the rickety
crib, the wood so gray it looks painted.
They've kept alert for snakes and rats.
The tears in their tee-shirts are mixed
blessings: when the breeze stirs, it puts
a cool stone against their sweat, but grit
clings fast at every opening, and horseflies
circle in. This crew has earned a trip to
town, and when they shoulder loudly
through the door and set their drinks on the
hot hood, it isn't white wine from Europe,
but something local, sweet, syrupy,
something they'll get sick on in the sun;
something darkly amber, slow enough
to smother every problem they have known.

When I saw the packaged bones of my
mother, I mourned her cold flight home,
locked away like baggage. She hadn't flown
in fourteen years. I worried about small things:
how long her polyester blouse would last,
how wrong it was to leave her glasses on.
I hated the stranger's hand that molded her
last look—the smile sinking like warm wax,
the face not hers, not mine, not anyone's.

Afterwards, I hunkered low,
mixing concrete to topcoat
my late grandmother's porch—
a storm-split trunk
had cracked the heart and
now the whole slab sagged.

But the wind crept up from
the empty lot across the way and
whirled above me in confusion.

What's all this? he asked.

Just a little home repair, I said—
no use in pointing fingers.

The wind spun itself down
to a small dust-devil and hovered.

What you're doing seems
odd to me, said the wind.

Well, some of us need shelter,
I explained, from cold and rain
and even from the likes of you.
We need a solid floor to walk on
and to hold our walls together.
We need a covering
to hide ourselves from sky.
But most of all we need a
level porch where we can sit
and think of abstract things.

No, I get all that, said the wind.
Being invisible doesn't mean
I'm blind. But I can tell you've
set about this work all wrong.

Like you would know, I said, and
troweled on a layer thick with lumps.

Oh, I'm quite familiar with construction,
said the wind. *I've lifted roofs and
toppled columns and leveled
the finest buildings of an age.
I've scoured away civilizations
so completely they've been lost to time.*

Good for you, I said.

The point, he huffed, *is I can spot
the makings of regret
looming from a mile away.*

Yeah, I said, everybody's an expert
on what someone else is doing.

Well, I'm no builder, I'll grant you that,
said the wind. *But your foundation
is obviously flawed. Without support
from underneath, whatever crack you
patch will open up again.*

You're immaterial, I pointed out.
What would you know about support?

I know the mechanics of force,
said the wind, lifting my ball cap
and cartwheeling it across the yard.
*So believe me when I say
the weight of this imperfect porch
foretells collapse.*

Leave me to my process, I replied.
Has it occurred to you that
my concern is not
to fix a failing porch?
That working on some solid thing
is just a way
to take me from myself?

No, said the wind, *those of us*
employed by natural law are numb
to what your feeble griefs might be.
We have continents to rearrange.

Then don't let me detain you, I said,

and as the blithe wind slipped away
over the hill, I scooped a fresh
trowel-full and slathered on
another coat, leaning my
accumulated weight over the crack
and pressing down with gravity.

The cold came hard, as always,
shivering the trees bare. I raked the
leaves and burned them. Now, after
three days, I scoop the remains into
plastic bags and sweep the oily residue
away. My hands are stained with ash.

Once, in the same span of days,
my mother died and was buried,
and each year I think there must be
something I should do. But my only
ritual is the rake, the fire, the broom.

There is no end to earthly disappearances.
My father, too, is gone, along with all my
elder kin. My own children look at me with
burdens beyond childhood in their eyes.

When I depart, the world will reinvent
itself and mysteries will multiply.

But that's not true. The mundane will hold
steady. Mail will pile up briefly with
my name. People will busy themselves
against the fall to no effect. Time will be
squandered on the rake, the fire, the broom.

The Night Marvin Gaye
Was Shot by His Father

We were four noisy punks in the heartland,
and March Madness was our main

preoccupation, a semi-final game, when
the stark news dragged across the screen.

Strange that it shocked us. As a species
we're prone to relative disasters. Nature

placed our eyes up front, looking forward,
so we can be blindsided daily; and though

there's never been a light as strong as
television, it can't illuminate that last

blood pulse before calamity. The glass
stays cool to the touch. Still, any one

of us could have warned him: success
is always booby-trapped. The other side

of *champion* is *defending champion*, and a
spot in the Top-40 doesn't mean much

at the kitchen table, where despair can
make us pull the trigger on anyone.

It doesn't matter what putty we started
out as. Babies lack vocabulary, but they

grasp well enough. When Great Aunt
Edith offers the blue ball in a voice

disguised as cartoon, we know that's not
the whole picture. The first rattle has no

snake attached, but others do, and before
long we're in math class dreaming 25 ways

to die tragically for love. It's not death
we crave, but the weeping afterwards.

I'm over fifty now. Age keeps me to the
sidewalks, and I move stiffly, eyes down,

the archivist headed for the library.
My thoughts stink like motel water.

I persist in my belief that all rickety
ladders are good for one last climb, but

someday I'll be wrong. If remorse were
a color it could fade in the dark. If remorse

were a door it could open partway. If
remorse were an ocean it would be no

different from what it's always been.
But if a fox can chew off its leg to get

away, so can anybody. Nothing separates
us from other animals except the rearview

mirror. The weatherman had called
for storms, but they'd blown through,

leaving a warm night. So we stepped
outside, picked our way through woods,

then across a field near the edge of the
quarry. We found a tall horse standing

in the dark pasture and pulled tangles
from its mane. We sang "Heard It Through

the Grapevine" loud enough to light
the distant farmer's window, and put

ourselves together again. We can outlive
certain things, but not our obligations,

not our reflections, not our shadows.
I will sit patiently while the sky guesses

my weight and rummage through a
history of small half-truths: the current

is always stronger than you think;
trees are taller at night; not all cats are

wise; the blue calm is deceptive at the edge
of the world, where some boats do sail off.

for Dean Young, Kevin Stein, and Ralph Burns

Dropping Dead in the Bathroom 1983

A guy gets up one morning
with a tick in his brain
that says Sunrise

he doesn't listen
just goes to brush his teeth

but the mirror cracks open
and between the shards
he sees himself

sitting on a park bench by the bay
it's a warm afternoon
salt spray soaks him to the skin

behind him on the dock
an old man plays a soft accordion

and the bones of drowned men
hungry for a tune
run slowly in to listen

Friends aren't what they used to be.
The circle has widened beyond all horizons,
and now people we don't know wander in
from the street to rummage through drawers
and stare into the refrigerator.

In this third year after her death, Claudia,
or the fact of her, prompted the ghosted
internet to tell the world that it's her birthday.
That's not inaccurate: beginnings are indelible.
But still. Old-fashioned friends, who know

a platform is no place to live, send love and
share the grief. But here and there among the
posts the clueless barge right in. *Do something
special today!* one tells her. *Have a fun week!*
says another. *Many happy returns!* Someone
sends a birthday song. A winking smiley face.

Claudia herself might have laughed off these
misplaced hints of immortality. But who's to say?

Every form of parchment fades in constant
light; what once was clear becomes illegible.
Now we see through a glass darkly but then
darker still. No doubt this same congratulation
will make the rounds again next year.

When you see it, remember the snuffed light of
blown-out candles. Think how much you've lost.

Day begins in silent gray, dank,
motionless, on the cool cusp
of autumn. No birds chirp.
The horses stare
toward the highway as morning
stagnates in the diffuse light.
A deep chill
ignites each supple branch.

Leaves begin their turn in a
multitude of signs, as green
becomes yellow, then red,
putting a natural stop to things.

Across the bitten field, logging
trucks drag their flaking haul
toward whatever comes next.

Sooner or later the moon will fall
to earth, but that's not our concern.
There's better news nearby:
the headwaters of the great river
start small, shallow enough to
wade across, and that's how it is
with every problem in the world.

But fall is a biased teacher.
The maple and the elm uncloak
to show that every song about life
is also a song about death.
The persimmon grows bitter,
and warns against the evergreen
optimism of spruce and pine,
hemlock and cedar, because the
killing frost is coming in, regardless.

But beware homilies from the plant
world. *Turn toward the light* sounds

fine at first, but we aren't daffodils.
How can we expose our backs
to darkness?
The days grow short, and color drains
away, returning to the earth through
that irresistible breakdown
we call decay. If nature is the mirror,
what's our way out?
That's the question in the cold, the one
that haunts us every circle of the sun.

We all struggle against the armed camp
of the psyche, negotiating treaties
with each turn of the head, each blink
of an eye. It isn't what we believe
that frightens us; it's everything else.

In a spiral true to the galaxy
of our birth, the world goes down,
and down,
and we change nothing.

And that's okay. One season calls up
curses from the dark, but others tell
a different tale. *Open your eyes,* they
say. *The moon is still up there, shining.*

Say it's come down
to the last few heartbeats
and you still don't have
an explanation: what then?

When you were six
you dropped a frog off a roof
to see if it enjoyed the jump—

even then haunted by
the things you would become.

Now there's no rescue.
You've lost your taste
for splashing into swamps,
for burying birds under bricks.
Everything you own
is useless.

The freckle-handed ladies
squint and nod.
They know you:
your handful of bright pebbles,
your empty house,
your skin still smooth as bone.

In the Last Smiling Photo
    of My Mother

2007

Fifty-five years old, she clutches
my father's arm for balance.
It's just before Christmas, no snow,
and they stand on the sidewalk
at the bottom of the front porch steps.

A tension rides the curve of their
shoulders, and they both look cold,
stiffened by a sudden wind.
May father's hands are shoved deep
in his pants pockets.

A wreath, black and receding
on the brickwork behind them,
floats above my mother's head.
Her white sweater and smooth slacks
seem borrowed, somehow, as if these
weren't the clothes she meant to wear.

Her blonde hair, what's left of it,
is combed forward like a child's,
and in this light seems almost cute,
not at all horrific. Her glasses
are large, bulbous, the strongest feature
on her face. She could be an owl.

No, not an owl—some smaller
crafted bird. A concrete likeness
frozen on a ledge, the base
now cracked, eyes wide, wings folded.

Oh, you again, I say.
The terror has worn thin.

Habit teaches us to live
with anything, I guess—
the way I stopped worrying
about the atomic bomb
in sixth grade after the
fiftieth false alarm, all us kids
huddled beneath our desks,
waiting for the final flash.

He leans on that famous scythe—
a habit of his own.
I think he carries it
only to scare the children,
to keep them out of reach.

Our routine is almost playful now.
Stop me if you've heard this,
he says. But he never stops.

*How many dead people does it take
to change a light bulb?*
He grins his trademark grin.
Irrelevant! he howls.
Their power's been cut off!
Then he cackles like a
drunken sorority pledge.

The humor, he believes,
lies not in the joke itself
but in the way he tells it.

He tells it repeatedly.

*How many dead people
does it take to change a lightbulb?*
he asks again.

This is the only joke he knows.
For him it never gets old.

But I surprise him.
Irrelevant! I interrupt.
The dead can't see the light.

Death gapes at me,
grinning uncertainly.

But then, inspired by the
breaking of fresh ground,
he tries a variation of his own.

Irrelevant! he cries. *The dead*
don't know what's watt!
He thinks he's hysterical
and laughs so hard
he unhinges his jaw.

How many dead people does it take,
he begins again.

This goes on for a while.
He's on a roll now, as
possibilities unfold without end.

I tell him I'm still listening,
that I've closed my eyes
only to concentrate
on his infinite comedic range.
I tell him his eternity of
punch lines is breathtaking.
I think he buys it.

How many dead people
does it take, he continues,

but I'm drifting away.

I ease down
through the sweetness
of the shadow.

Words release me
from their mystery,

and I sink, dreamless,
toward the usual slumber,

forgetting the joke entirely.

My daughter calls to ask me questions
for a survey in her college class:

> *Can you name something*
> *meaningful you've lost?*

Interpreting my silence as a blank,
she tries to help: *It can be anything,*
she tells me, *even a lost shirt.*

She doesn't understand the scope of
what she asks. I'm fifty-four; I've killed
more sacred things than I can name.

Has she noticed, I wonder, how
disjunctive the world can be, that the
heart is not heart-shaped after all?

> *The past,*

I offer, finally, and feel her frown.
That doesn't work, she says. *It ruins*
what comes next. I know she's right.

But later she calls again, my second chance.

> *Have you tried to replace it?*

she asks. This time I skip the silence,
slide straight into a string of useless
blather. Somehow not a word of it is
>   *no.*

I'll start with a fact:
Billy Faught died in a war.

That Billy's last name was Faught
is something too heavy-handed for fiction,
where the author gets to make such choices.
But I have no choice here.
Billy's last name was Faught.

There's no interesting or exciting story
about the Viet Cong firing on his helicopter.
The report offers no vivid sensory details to
make the experience of his death come alive.
I can't say what happened
because I wasn't there.

But here are some details that survive,
paltry as they are,
some from the official record,
some from what I know:

Billy was a year and five months older,
but we were in the same draft lottery—
the first since World War II—
and boys of both our ages
were being swept up.
His number was 117, mine was 122,
and that was the slim difference between us.

Maybe he enlisted when his number hit,
hoping to improve his odds
of landing a plum assignment.
Or maybe he waited until they called him up
and just let the chips fall.
Maybe he'd have joined anyway,
whatever his number,
for pure love of country.
I don't know.
Was he anxious? Excited? Fatalistic?

I have no idea.
Whatever his circumstance,
he began his tour of duty on
May 26th, 1970, when he was nineteen.

I was eighteen, finishing high school,
having the time of my life.
My draft number was borderline,
but I kept my fingers crossed.
Things looked good for my deferment:
I'd been accepted into college.
My girlfriend was a blond cheerleader
who said she'd marry me
if I got sent to Viet Nam.

I don't know if Billy had a girlfriend.

My great-aunt may have told me once
that Billy had a pregnant wife,
but I'm not sure, time having left
so many thick clouds on the horizon.
But that would explain a lot.
With a family to support,
he'd have likely dropped out of school,
and Selective Service always
moved in fast on boys like that.
But I don't know.
Maybe there was no wife, no child.
Maybe there was no one.

Billy snagged a job
that should have kept him safe:
helicopter mechanic.
Not part of the crew,
just someone who repaired problems
back at the base.

The date of his *incident*—
which is the term the Army uses—

was July 25th, 1970, just two months in.
I was probably playing golf,
going to the movies, having fun.
It was my last summer
before leaving home.

Specialist Fourth Class Billy Faught
died in Bien Hoa Province,
and his body was recovered.
His *casualty type*—
another term the Army uses—
was *non-hostile*.
Non-hostile, it reads.
Died of other causes.

Further down the form,
under *casualty detail*,
there's no detail at all,
just a category:
air loss over land.

In four subsequent categories,
the designations read:
was not MIA
was not MIA
was not MIA
was not MIA
Simple words repeated
like a grade-school primer.

To most people Arlington, Virginia,
means the cemetery
where so many of our soldiers rest.
But Billy had a native claim
on Arlington. He was born there.
He grew up there. He could see
the Washington Monument from his yard.

Here's one possibility:
Billy was working on the ground
when a damaged helicopter,
struggling to make it back to base,
fell on him from the sky.

Here's another possibility:
Billy took a ride
in a damaged helicopter
to assess repairs.
It fell with him inside.

I prefer the second version,
the one that, for a brief time,
lifts Billy up.

The first version curses me:
I can see Billy chopped apart
by helicopter blades
as he tries to run for cover.
Now I've burdened you with that image,
even though I can tell you plainly
it's pure imagination.
I don't know what happened.
I wasn't there.
I've never been there.

But there are places I've been,
places all over the country,
all over the world.
One of those places,
one of the most important,
was Arlington, Virginia, when I was five.
Billy lived in the building next door
and had already started first grade.
There's not much I can say about the boy.
He was bigger than I was, of course,
but his size was normal for his age.
I think he had brown hair.

I know that he was nice.
I know that for the two years I was there
he stuck by me, a solid pal.

I told him I was afraid to go to school
because I couldn't read—
and from what I understood,
reading was something that went on there.
So Billy said he'd teach me how,
and every day we huddled over the pages
of his book—*Fun With Dick and Jane*—
as he moved his fingers over the letters,
sounding out the simple repetition of
simple words until I knew enough
to say them for myself.

Billy opened a door,
and I passed through into a world
of Dick and Jane,
Baby Sally and their dog, Spot.
There may have been a cat named Puff,
though memory across so many years
allows me little certainly.

In any case, through Billy's heart
I learned to read, and since that time
I've read a hundred thousand tales.
That's more than Milton ever read,
and more than Shakespeare.
Nothing special about it, though—
we're in an age of access.
We can read anything we think to look for.

So here I am.
My lengthening trail of words
has circled back and brought me
to a place I never wished to be:
Billy's own last page,
a bureaucratic log

on a government web site,
a bundle of bare facts
fastened to a name
carved on the Memorial Wall:
Panel 8, Line 51:
William Avener Faught, Jr.

Some facts, of course, go unrecorded.
Our favorite page showed Dick
sailing his toy plane on the wind.
It soared away from him into a blue sky
while Jane and Sally watched in awe.
Up, up, said Baby Sally. *Go up, up, up.*

When something unnatural burns,
the smell can't help but bring suspicion:
acrid smoke might mean the worst.

Normally I'd worry, but not this time.
Neighbors cackle out conversation
across the road, and a diversity of birds

chatters unalarmed above the weedy,
hard-baked ground. Unlooked for, a
memory shivers loose from the trees,

shrugging off more weight than
half a century, and suddenly I'm back
where I started, in a time when other

birds chirped, a blue breeze shifted, and
that same stink drifted in from the fire pit
out back, where castoffs of our daily life

were fed to flames, their forms darkening
from every bright color into ash, harmless,
we believed, as the dusty light slanting

through the living room. I can feel the
bristled rug beneath my knees, see
my grandmother's marble-topped tables,

ashtrays everywhere, a wind-up clock
on the granite mantle above the
granite hearth, roses on the wallpaper,

my parents smiling their happy-family
smiles from the crackling plastic of
the couch, still immune to life's most

catastrophic ends. Cicadas beyond
the black screen door whir through
the sluggish afternoon, and my

great-grandfather blesses us at
dinnertime with his mumbled prayer,
then beats me at checkers afterwards.

They all had some last thing to say,
I guess, but nothing stuck. Now I'm
their only trace. Gradually, I've slipped

inside the stitching of lost ancestors,
layering them over me like hand-me-
down clothes. What here is solely mine?

Or am I just a bulk inheritance of genes,
the pieces of my puzzle jigsawed from
bygone versions of myself? Our self.

When I bend to watch a praying mantis
scale a stalk of golden rye, am I the
prehistoric one? The medieval one?

The one who doctored Andrew Jackson
in the sad war against the Creeks?
The one who lost his printing press

to General Sherman on his march?
The one whose honeymoon ended in the
great San Francisco earthquake and fire?

More likely, I'm the multitudes I'll never
know—farmers, firemen, horse thieves,
midwives, preachers, beggars, kings.

They linger in the way my hand grips
an axe, a spoon, a steering wheel;
in the way my brow furrows at a leaky

roof or limbs creaking in a gale. They
linger in my fear of dark alleys, my hatred
of the cold, my taste for turnip greens.

More and more my answer to the dead
is *Oh, I see.* My answer to the rest of
us is silence, awkward and tomblike.

My father, who flew bombing runs
in World War II, once told me he had
heard a pilot's final words: *Uh-oh,*

the boy had said, and that's about as
universal as it gets. In the end, we all
want to do our family proud, we all want

to spend that last breath blurting some
brilliant p.s. they'll be quoting in the high
schools. Who wouldn't want to cry out

something never said before, something
that identifies the rank genesis of all our
longing? But let's face it, some things

are easier done than said. I do believe it's
out there, the answer to the unarticulated
mystery, written into everything we know—

earth, air, water, fire, time's most antique
alphabet. But knowledge is a labyrinth
with no exit strategy. Who can read signs

in the garden at midnight? Who can stand
before the blank chalkboard and explain
things to the class? At odd times, alone

beside a mailbox, or in a car, or even
in a dream, I feel as if I've come within
arm's length of the unnamable, believe

myself balanced on the verge of
comprehending that the white stone is
not just the white stone, but is also the

scuffed root arching above the broken
earth, the brittle veins of last year's leaf,
the ant racing along the porch boards,

the vanished wind catching its own
breath, the burst of flowers—yellow,
purple, red—in the greening corner pot,

the solid shape of everything around me,
the thoughts that even now ignite new
brushfires in the dry wilds of my brain.

Friend, when I'm done with oxygen and
blood, speechless, not another word
to my name, please do me the kindness

of assuming I was finally there, lounging
at the nexus, when death stepped in; that
the material and the immaterial coalesced;

that diamonds dissipated into pure ideas
while pure ideas became diamonds.
But don't oversell it; don't say that

someone seeded the clouds with angels
and the sky rained proverbs without
number; don't say that language

geysered up from the dark, flooding the
earth with light, spilling all secrets,
washing all consequences away. I may go

quietly, or not; singing, raving, or flinging
vile curses at the nurse. So forget last
words. It's enough if what I find upon

leaving is a fresh start, or at least a
fresh perspective, or even just one split
second free of all loneliness and regret.

A green field, a yellow sun, a rabbit in the
morning brush, a baseball nestled in a glove;
anything but the nothing of a black sky. Give

me anything, and I'll call it a fair exchange,
equal in value to all the time I spent wondering
in this charred and ever-changing land.

Will the Last to Leave
Please Turn out the Lights

It starts with a road, whether you call it that or not.
There's sunshine, the first trick of happiness;
darkness, the first misgiving.
Things appear and disappear,
brought and taken by the road,
and you realize your wishes are not law.

You give in to growth: adjust, suppress.
You watch the road. Before long you take a step,
and then there's nothing left but progress,
wagonloads of it, filled with shoes and toasters,
pay stubs and mandolins, all heading for the dump.

Obligation plants its flag.
You feed the beasts in the yard,
douse each unattended campfire,
keep track of your appointments.
Remembering becomes your burden,
relentless, the clock on the bedside table
ticking through the night.

In time you see that time is just a storehouse,
that the road is nothing without the traveler,
that time is nothing without the road.

But no one untangles a knot by pulling it tighter,
so let's put all our sacred -isms in the yard sale pile.
Loosen the noose, unclench the fist;
stop fabricating enemies.
Reality is guesswork to the physicist
but not to you and me. We know
which hand holds the cleaver, which the meat.
We know that sometimes a bad diagnosis
is a step in the right direction.

Eternity is always there, whistling us home,
but we're the disobedient dog, distracted
by some vague scent in the wilderness.
We build prisons and churches for the lost,

and cross our fingers for the rest.
We nurture one persistent hope: that the mind
is a jar sturdy enough to survive the journey,
no matter the weather, no matter the road.

Enjoy whatever doesn't last:
carnivals and red dwarf stars, fireflies and wisdom.
Stop whining about chipped glassware
and missed phone calls—
even the potentate knows disappointment.
Sure, we lost the last set of keys.
We broke too many hearts in selfish ignorance,
wore the wrong socks to the dance,
ignored those late-night ads for saving children.
In the larger scheme, we may already be extinct.

But the wheel will turn again, as it always does.
New hills will rise, new fields will fill the plains;
and on some distant unencumbered dawn,
we'll rise into the light of our potential.
We'll enter every door a stranger
bringing offerings of bread and wine.
We'll sing off-key without regret.
We'll make no promises.
We'll get things right the next time.

Clint McCown has published four novels and five previous volumes of poems. The only two-time recipient of the American Fiction Prize, he has also received the Midwest Book Award, the Sister Mariella Gable Prize, the Society of Midland Authors Award, the Germaine Breé Book Award, an NEA grant, an Academy of American Poets Prize, a Barnes & Noble Discover Great New Writers designation, and a Distinction in Literature citation from the Wisconsin Library Association. In journalism, he received an Associated Press Award for Documentary Excellence for his investigations of organized crime and political corruption. He has worked as a screenwriter for Warner Bros. and as a Creative Consultant for HBO television. He is a former principal actor with the National Shakespeare Company, and several of his plays have been produced. His poems, essays, and stories have appeared widely. He has edited a number of literary magazines, including the *Indiana Review* and the *Beloit Fiction Journal*, which he founded in 1984. He currently directs the MFA program at Virginia Commonwealth University and teaches in the low-residency MFA program at the Vermont College of Fine Arts.